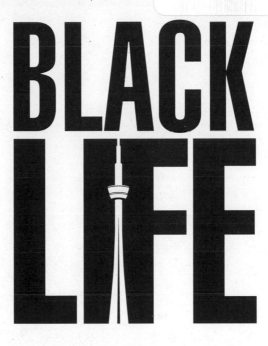

BLACK LIFE

POST-BLM AND THE STRUGGLE FOR FREEDOM

Rinaldo Walcott and Idil Abdillahi

ARP BOOKS • WINNIPEG

ARP Books (Arbeiter Ring Publishing)
205-70 Arthur Street
Winnipeg, Manitoba
Treaty 1 Territory and Historic Métis Nation Homeland
Canada R3B 1G7
arpbooks.org

Cover design and layout by Mike Carroll.
Printed and bound in Canada by Friesens on paper made from
100% recycled post-consumer waste.

ARP Books acknowledges the generous support of the Manitoba Arts Council and the Canada
Council for the Arts for our publishing program. We acknowledge the financial support of the
Government of Canada through the Canada Book Fund and the Province of Manitoba through
the Book Publishing Tax Credit and the Book Publisher Marketing Assistance Program of
Manitoba Culture, Heritage, and Tourism.

LIBRARY AND ARCHIVES CANADA CATALOGUING IN PUBLICATION

Library and Archives Canada Cataloguing in Publication

Title: BlackLife : post-BLM and the struggle for freedom / Rinaldo Walcott & Idil
    Abdillahi.
Names: Walcott, Rinaldo, 1965- author. | Abdillahi, Idil, author.
Description: Includes bibliographical references.
Identifiers: Canadiana (print) 20190094885 | Canadiana (ebook) 20190094923 |
    ISBN 9781927886212 (softcover) | ISBN 9781927886243 (ebook)
Subjects: LCSH: Blacks—Canada—Social conditions. | LCSH: Racism—Canada. |
    LCSH: Canada—Race relations.
Classification: LCC FC106.B6 W35 2019 | DDC 305.896/071—dc23

BlackLife:
Post-BLM and
the Struggle for Freedom

Contents

for Yusra Khogali

Acknowledgments

We have made BlackLife one word because we believe that living Black makes BlackLife inextricable from the mark of its flesh, both historically and in our current time. The mark of Black flesh is the foundation from which BlackLife in all of it multiplicities, varieties, potentialities and possibilities proceeds from and is therefore intimately entangled.

We wish to thank our multiple interlocutors who have engaged us on the ideas in these pages in many different venues. Many of these ideas began as blog posts and became conference papers but most significantly, for the most part, these ideas have been mulled over time and again over drinks and food at various venues in Toronto. We thank our friends for enabling, listening, challenging, sharing, responding and supporting.

Introduction:
The Black 1990s, or How BlackLife Came to Matter

The beginning and end points of what happens in these pages are 1992 and 2005. In 1992, Black young people and others rioted on Yonge Street in Toronto. The protest against police violence erupted into anger, expressed largely with the destruction of property. Shortly thereafter, the Stephen Lewis report on race relations in Ontario (1992), was issued, and a series of social programs were initiated to address poverty, employment and other concerns that faced the Black community. In 2005, after a rash of gun violence often largely affecting young Black people, the mainstream media dubbed the period "the summer of the gun." In that instance, the state responded with the Toronto Anti-Violence Intervention Strategy (TAVIS). TAVIS was a special division of the Toronto Police

Services, created to police what have come to be called "priority neighbourhoods" in Toronto. "Priority neighbourhood" is a euphemism for non-white, poor or working class areas where a large percentage of the population are Black people.

Across Canada, in any large urban area where Black people live the same dynamics are at play. This book speaks from the geopolitics of Toronto, but its insights have implications far beyond Toronto. The reality is that BlackLife in Canada finds itself being expressed and circumscribed by the demand from Black people that it be a full life and resisted by a set of forces, structures and people that it be something less than a full life. *BlackLife* then seeks to speak to the complicated dynamics of Black self-assertion and anti-Black racism in Canada.

In retrospect, we now know it was the end, even if it felt like the beginning back then. The 1990s in Canada were Black. The 1990s marked the full emergence of Black cultural politics in Canada in a manner that had not previously existed. In film, music, literature, visual arts and theatre, Black Canada asserted itself, indelible evidence of its presence in the nation. The 1990s marked a significant and important period of Black Canadian artistic production and activism that many assumed would produce a changed political and cultural landscape. Black Canadian contributions would proliferate across multiple spheres, institutions and cultural genres, changing the Canadian landscape indelibly and maybe even enshrining an authentic representation of our avowed multicultural present. Alas, such desires never came to fruition, and the Canadian landscape that might authentically come close to representing our multicultural demographics remains elusive still.

Nineteen ninety-five was quite the year. Mike Harris and the Ontario Progressive Conservative party's forming the new provincial government signalled the beginning of the end of Black possibilities in a number of ways. Belatedly, we might now understand the moment as one when the full effects of neoliberal economic and cultural reorganizing announced itself in what was then understood as Canada's most important province, Ontario, and definitely its most important city, Toronto. The effects of this period on public policy are still being experienced and reckoned with today. By 1999, at the end of the Harris era, all of the ingredients necessary for Black people's deepening marginalization, displacement and permanent exclusion had been cemented into place.

Taken from the vantage point of cultural expression, the effects of the period remain with us still. For example, Andrea Fatona (2011) in "Where Outreach Meets Outrage": Racial Equity at The Canada Council for the Arts (1989–1999), an important dissertation that has marked the period 1989 to 1999 as one not only of artists' activism that changed the cultural landscape, but also, simultaneously saw the waning of the promise for Black artists' production. In her research she demonstrates how Black cultural producers' activism, in coalition with other non-white artists and activists, produced a racial equity landscape for arts and culture that began to wane in the Harris years in Ontario, and nationally in the Paul Martin years, when he served as finance minister in Jean Chretien's Liberal government. These are the years of Canadian structural adjustment, then referred to as "deficit reduction." The former term is usually reserved for global south economies. The impact of deficit reduction on cultural production in this country interrupted a more fulsome racial equitable representative output, one that was significantly hampered by the economic and social policies of that very brutal governmental period.

Instead, we want to think here both temporally and nostalgically about the cultural context of Black Canada's "arrival," but as well about the lost opportunities that have never been fully achieved by us. Back then, we danced to Maestro Fresh Wes letting our backbone slide; heard Liberty Silver croon in jazz and supper clubs; the Dream Warriors exploded in Europe with their cool, inflected, jazzy hip hop; Devon called on us "to keep up the pressure" in his song and video, "Mr. Metro," about anti-Black police violence; Acid Jazz Wednesdays at Cameron House were lit; the late Austin Clarke returned to the literary scene; Dionne Brand emerged as one of our most important poets; Djanet Sears owned the theatre stages; dub poetry and its practitioners howled Black resistance—this was the Black 1990s and it seemed, then, like it would continue in perpetuity.

What we hope to show in *BlackLife* is how to think about Black Canadian life, cultural expression and its archives that are both nationally bound and locally articulated, as in the specificity of Toronto, and yet still exceed the national, in as Black diasporic concerns with freedom. We see this in the hairstyles, the language, the proverbs and of course the trouble of policing: all point to ongoing national, local and diasporic experiences of BlackLife. We hint in these pages that BlackLife and the political concerns for Black people in Canada are globally oriented and still experienced in their local-national formation too.

The Black 1990s came to a crushing end with the full on assault of neoliberal policies that impacted everything from education to housing to the arts and beyond. What remained were issues like over policing, crime and ongoing degradations of BlackLife. The "summer of the gun" in 2005 firmly cemented Black disregard in the nation-state of Canada by gesturing in so many ways to the permanency of Black exclusion and subjection. The Black 1990s is owed a debt, one that Canada needs to pay in full and one that BlackLife grapples to extract from the state and its extra-state apparatus.

1

Slavery's Afterlife in Canada: Anti-Blackness and Late Modernity's Enduring Racial Violence

To excavate coloniality, then, one must always include and analyze the project of modernity, although the reverse is not true, because coloniality points to the absences that the narrative of modernity produces (Walter Mignolo, *The Idea of Latin America*, p.xii-xiii, 2005).

The colonist bourgeois, in its narcissistic dialogue, expounded by the members of its universities, had in fact deeply implanted in the minds of the colonized intellectual that the essential qualities remained eternal in spite of all the blunders men may make: the essential qualities of the West, of course (Frantz Fanon, *The Wretched of the Earth*, p.46).

In that context then, it is important to give similar recognition to the kind of intellectual work produced organically outside the academy and accord that work the same weight and space one gives to academic production (Carole Boyce Davies, *Left of Karl Marx: The Political Life of Black Communist Claudia Jones*, p.10).

For the Black, freedom is an ontological, rather than experiential, question (Frank B. Wilderson, *Red, White and Black: Cinema and the Structure of U.S. Antagonisms*).

On *Fire and Glory*, an album by Kardinal, there is a track called "Freshie," in which the rapper narrates the migration of Freshie from Kingston, Jamaica and his becoming a "gangsta." As Kardinal tells us, Freshie's mom was working overtime, two jobs; and Freshie was at home hungry "on the block with no food to eat." His choice was then to become a "gangsta." The song narrates Freshie's involvement in street crime and the price he ultimately pays for it. It is notable for its analysis of the ways in which Kardinal economically produces a musical text that documents how certain situations come to be, that is the dangerous labour left for Black men that we have come to call "drug dealing," "street crime," "hustling" and other euphemisms. Kardinal documents the ways in which the conditions of poverty, migration, under-employment and the breakdown in familial relations, alongside youths' ability to convince their parents of that which they do not want to see, all produced Freshie as a "gangsta," or what Wilderson calls "the gratuitous violence" of BlackLife, is produced. And even when Freshie is deported to Jamaica he makes a return migration and eventually suffers "fatal wounds to the back of the head" in Canada, at the hands of the police.

On *Fire and Glory*, Kardinal rhymes about a number of situations deeply pertinent to the contemporary conditions of the Black poor and of urban life in the early moments of the 21st century. The album is among a number of artistic interventions by Black Canadians across a range of genres that attempt to intervene into what we call the enduring and continuing legacy of modernity's anti-Black violence and crime. Central to this legacy of violence and crime are the conditions under which migrations both historically and presently occur for Black peoples and their relationship to both historical and present global and local economic conditions. A subtext of this chapter is the post-Columbus contemporary migrations that are a significant aspect of the structure of anti-blackness and thus require thought in any politics that seeks to dismantle such structures. The central theme of the chapter would be to think through the ways in which Black peoples' lives, especially those of poor Black people, offer us the opportunity to think about the consequences of what Langston Hughes once called "vicious modernism." In order to do so, we tackle as a secondary line of thought the terms of how the structures of anti-blackness, and the politics of migration, aid in the potential to produce a decolonial desire and a possible decolonial future. It is our argument that merely pointing to the work of anti-blackness is not sufficient, therefore, however risky, a decolonial utterance is necessary too. Thus, this chapter is an inquiry into how knowledges and ideas continue to extend and produce forms of violence and indeed actions of crime in the lives of what, following Nas, Sylvia Wynter and Frantz Fanon, I now call "global niggerdom"—the starving, the jobless, the HIV/AIDS infected, the police (quo state) brutalized, those armed to kill their likeness and so on.

Global niggerdom finds its historical development in the crucible of coloniality/modernity's real gift to us—that of violence and crime enacted on the Black body (but not exclusively) nonetheless we must be clear that colonial-modernity produced the Black body as a non-body that might endure its most brutal inventions. Therefore, this chapter is a kind of call to scholars to undo, at least the "narratively condemned status of the black" (Wynter, 1994) in our work so that other imaginings might not only be possible but could also become evident. Anti-blackness seems to be the force that prohibits more radical re-orderings of our world. To do so we must rethink all that the modern/colonial world, as Mignolo would have it, has bequeathed to us.

To suggest that modernity is constituted fundamentally of violence and what we might call crime, might strike some as a solipsistic assault on what is considered one of Europe's most important contributions to human culture. However, we come to the position of engaging modernity's violence and crime from a different school of thought. Deeply influenced by Edward Said, in particular *Culture and Imperialism*, and Toni Morrison's *Playing in the Dark*, we are interested in what Paul Gilroy called the "counter-cultures of modernity." This is not an anti-modern exercise we are about to embark on, but rather a critical engagement and counter-discourse of or to modernism's ideals and ideas as those ideals remain elusive for many, both material and immaterial realities. This is particularly important in the context of our late modernity where discourses of freedom, civil rights, human rights and cultural rights have come to occupy the "secularly scared" place of Euro-American modernity's crumbling present and future. Before we begin to grapple with the meaning of that crumbling future it is worth repeating the conditions under which modernity's claims for a different kind of human is bequeathed to us—the only view offered to us.

In Toni Morrison's contrapuntal reading of the Enlightenment, she reminded us some time ago in *Playing in the Dark*, that "The slave population, it could be and was assumed, offered itself up as surrogate selves for meditation on problems of human freedom, its lure and its elusiveness" (p.37). She further adds, "we should not be surprised that the Enlightenment could accommodate slavery; we should be surprised if it had not. The concept of freedom did not emerge in a vacuum. Nothing highlighted freedom—if it did not in fact create it—like slavery" (p.38). Morrison's comments can be situated in the evidence of New World slavery and Indigenous colonialization, which constitute the "violent origins" as Spivak (1993) once named them, of the foundations of the unfolding of modernity as both a philosophical invention and as a set of material, cultural, economic, political and social positions and conditions under which all of human life was reorganized under the parochialism of Europe's world view. Both Edward Said and Sylvia Wynter have taught us how to both decipher and analyze how Europe's partial view of the world has come to be the dominant view of the world.

Following Wynter then, one of the principle attributes of European modernity that we must grapple with continually is its initial movement of people around the globe in ways that disrupted previous settlements of those peoples. Such movements that we now call migration are founded in anti-blackness, taking their logic from transatlantic slavery. Thus, it is our contention that the politics and logics of contemporary immigration have embedded in them anti-Black logics. This can be noticed in the simple fact of moving "labour" to sites of production as transatlantic slavery so glaringly inaugurated on a mass scale. The movement of people that we might call slavery, Indigenous colonization and displacement, European resettlement, indentureship and so on in historical moments, goes by other names today. Today we speak of immigrants or immigration; guest workers or various kinds of worker pro-grams; 'illegal aliens', their undocumented/non-status, genera-tions of immigrant children and so on. But all of these terms reference some kind of movement and reordering of the globe under Europe's terms or conditioned by those terms. Thus, movement as a condition, even more than a practice, is fun-damental to modernity in its very conception and its practices and based in Black debasement. As Said points out, it was in fact the "overseas departments" (as the French like to think of them) that produced the resources to provide the time and space for the developments of the ideas and ideals of modernity and more specifically its material advancements and social and political organization. Said's point is a different take on the Morrison quote we offered earlier.

Significantly, migration, then, is a crucial element of modernity and not an outcome of it as some scholars seem or want to suggest. Embedded in that actual movement and real politics of migration is the simultaneous construction and production of Europe's invention, ordering, cataloguing and naming of people, places and things according to its own views of the world. A significant element of Europe's modernity is the production of types, especially, by race, sex, gender and culture, which are all also conceived as outside blackness, thus constituting a foundational anti-Black modernism. All those categories are rarified in European modernity, and while deeply troubling, nonetheless those same categories are contradictorily also deeply meaningful for many in a post-1492 world.

HISTORIZING THE MODERN AS A PROBLEM AND WRITING SLAVERY INTO IT

Since 1492, the globe has been embroiled in a conception of the human driven by European man-human conceptuality, understandings and categorizations of the world and thus the globe. The conception of the human that European Enlightenment bequeaths us, and which is then fine-tuned in early modernity as a product of colonial governance in a world reordered under European forms of culture, politics and economics, and enforced by the gun—is the foundation upon which the trouble and necessity of thinking differently about the politics of knowledge rests. But if 1492 is a material and symbolic unfolding of European conceptions of the world on their own cosmo-political terms, then post-World War Two ushers in other opportunities through anticolonial struggles, civil rights movements, feminisms and gay and lesbian liberation. These movements both desire and shore up the full occupation of the extension of Europe's Enlightenment project to finally inaugurate the fulfillment of European conceptions of the man-human paradigm and simultaneously call that project into profound questioning.

By the man-human paradigm we mean to suggest the foundational premise of Euro-political religio-philosophical orientation, which understands the human as a category always already gendered as man, raced as white and sexualized as heterosexual and never Black. This reigning conception of man-human has been at the root of post-1492 conceptions of community, in which philoso-political struggles of various kinds—anticolonial, feminists, gay and lesbian and anti-racist have demanded and to some measure forced revisions of the man-human conception, demonstrating its flexibility by adding to it and elaborating it, but not changing in any radical sense its foundational claim as the only way of conceiving of human life. Thus, all other conceptions of human life have been subsumed into the European man-human conception or dismissed as not relevant. Non-European conceptions of the human therefore hold very little sway and understanding in most of our political and scholarly discourses today. We all live various versions of European coloniality/

modernity regardless of what claims we might make on behalf of other forms of knowing and living.

As both the engines and the disposable excess of early and late industrial capitalism and modernity, Black people and coloured bodies have a particular and specific mark within the contexts of global relations. Without rehearsing the massive debates concerning the place of the Black diaspora and other diasporas like the Asian in early and late capitalism and modernity and late modernity, it should suffice to say for now, that these diasporas are the B-side of globalization discourses, as I have argued elsewhere (Walcott, 2006). While I do not intend to suggest that there are no critical and doubtful critiques of globalization discourses in the academy, what remains interesting are the ways in which a particular racial divide exists around how the global is invoked. To put it crudely, white folks *do* globalization and folks of colour *do* diaspora or white folks invoke the global as a necessary good, forgetting how much of it is undergirded by brutal forms of violence and death—Black death. This is a divide that we need to pay much attention to, because we think that it demands a return to the "old" politics of representation and the desire to constitute communities of the same that belie the difficult political lives that we all live, that is to a time before liberal multicultural politics. It too easily opens up the space for innocent and guilty locations, and the artists we shall discuss below eschew such designations. It is a space that critiques of identity politics have taught us to doubt, but it also does not allow for moving to the site or at least the more difficult tasks of the ethical imperative to produce a different world now.

Paul Gilroy's writing in the context of a new postcolonial Europe allows us to see how the spectres of global "raciology," (*Against*, 2000) as he calls it, inform his analysis. In delineating the modern global terms of modernist raciology Gilroy writes of a counterhistory: "At the very least it demands a comprehensive rethinking of the impact of the brutal market activity in human beings which culminated in coffee, sugar, chocolate and tea, not to mention new forms of banking, insurance and governmental administration, becoming familiar—even essential—elements in the common European habitus" ("The Sugar", 2000, p.127) — echoing and extending Fanon's observation in *Wretched of the Earth* (p.96). This continuing disappearing history of postmodern globalization drags the old questions of representation back to the fore. But we also know that these old questions of representation cannot be taken up as if those who were colonized represent innocent subjects in the technological, governmental mechanisms of global capital now. Thus, we are faced with two imperatives cogently articulated by Gilroy. We must engage "an ethical dimension to action against racial injustice and its hierarchies" ("The Sugar", 2000, p.128) and we must inquire, "into an ethical, less market driven multiculturalism" (p.129).

What does it mean to create knowledge in a post-slavery world? How might we begin to acknowledge, as Nas brilliantly points out on his now famous untitled album, that we are all living in the throes of "post-traumatic slave syndrome"? By this we mean the ongoing terror of the afterlife of slavery that continues to structure and produce, in both psychic and material ways, the violence at both micro and macro levels that produces Black death. It seems to me that as scholars of the humanities and social sciences we must and should concern ourselves with the conditions of the writing of knowledge, given how its production is implicated in the ruling and regulating of social behaviour and the production of sociality. We live in an era where knowledge is readily contested and a multiplicity of ways of knowing are asserted—this is no longer surprising to most—for if the present moment characterizes anything it is the collapse of Eurocentred grand narratives of mankind and universality and the proliferation and dissemination of counter-narratives to articulate new conceptions of what Sylvia Wynter (1992) calls "a new science of human forms of life" (p.240). But while the collapse has been inaugurated in the academy, the orienting signs and practices of the past remain brutal real-world experiences for Black peoples, as evidenced by let's say policing, but it could be healthcare too, for examples.

The artists we will discuss echo what Zygmunt Bauman has termed "wasted lives," and they all attempt to "write" the narrative of such lives as not the excess of our time, but rather as produced in and by the violence and crime of it, and they do so ethically as a challenge to the ideals of modernity. While Bauman is concerned to assess wasted lives in terms of environmental waste, he is also interested in the conditions which have produced wasted lives for migrants, refugees and other outcasts. In this particular historical moment the people that the artists speak with and yes, maybe even for, constitute the outcasts. Bauman reads globalization as producing various kinds of waste, chief among them wasted humans. Shortly, we will turn to reading how these wasted populations provide us with a sense of what is at stake in their relation to late modernity. We specifically ask questions about how human waste is being produced in Canada, as Canada participates as one node in this global circuit of late transnational capitalism.

A shift occurs in post-World War Two logics of the human; it is a shift that must contend with the human's remaking as a new human on the basis of consumption, especially in the West. Thus, Bauman writes, "consumers are the prime assets of consumer society; flawed consumers are its most irksome and costly liabilities" (p.39). One might here think of the London Riots in 2011 where so much coverage was about poor people "looting shops" in the aftermath of the murder of a Black man, Mark Duggan, by police; (Ferguson, USA erupted similarly in the aftermath of the execution of 18-year-old Mike Brown by police). Crucial to this remaking were, and remain with us still, the production of utopian futures made possible by ever-increasing technological inventions which would supposedly free humans from the drudgery of everyday life.

Therefore, we would suggest that one of the triumphs of neoliberal ideologies has been its very effective management (not efficient as it likes to claim and we can see everywhere today) of the imagination, right alongside economy, institutions, populations and so on. An effective element of that managerialism has been the production of wasted populations or as the LAPD put it in the time of Rodney King NHI (No Humans Involved). Wynter made a call in both a 1984 essay and then more than a decade later in "No Humans Involved: Open Letter to My Colleagues"; she wrote, "I propose[d] that the task of black studies, together with those of all the other new studies that entered the academy in the wake of the 1960s uprisings, should be that of rewriting knowledge" (p.16). As Wynter laments in 1994, such a project has barely gotten off the ground, and in 2014 it remains the same for the foreseeable future. Instead, humanist and social scientists have found themselves mired in a repetitive cycle of disciplinary boundary keeping. Disciplinary boundary keeping of the worst kind has inhibited our ability to engage critically with and produce the conditions for new imaginative worlds. Too few scholars risk thinking critically and imaginatively about liberal democracies, and too few of us are willing to articulate or imagine worlds other than those we have experienced. Instead our radical stance seems to be suggesting momentarily short-circuiting what we presently have as if such short-circuiting can effectively interrupt the death drives of capitalism and liberal democracy's relentless drive to make Black personhood disappear globally. In the face of mounting and ever-growing evidence of the now global Black archipelagoes of poverty, the desire to dream and reflect new contexts for human possibilities has fallen entirely on the intellectual shoulders of artists, we would argue. Or at least the ethical pause to make us think differently about our present and future now lies with artists.

REWRITING GENRES OF MAN:
DIONNE BRAND AND AUSTIN CLARKE

Wynter's call for new kinds of knowledges takes its answer in the literature, among other genres of the Black diaspora that we are most familiar with. Dionne Brand has been writing about the migratory experience since 1983 with her *Winter Epigrams: & Epigrams to Ernesto Cardenal in Defense of Claudia*, and over that time the politics of movement has changed and evolved from the invocation of the cold and frigid to one in which alienation, celebration, pain, shame and pleasure live up close to each other and even inside each other, all of them markers of Black terror and violence enacted on Black people. In this way, Brand's poetry, fiction and essays chronicle a very specific history of yet another temporal shift in post-World War Two global migrations, that of the 60s and 70s. Brand chronicles the economies of migratory urban life with a language evocative of the tight spaces we negotiate in cities as blackness is spectacularized. Brand's work allows us to see the conditions of global niggerdom through a politics of migration as one lens.

From Brand's *Thirsty*

> History doesn't enter here, life, if you call it that
>
> on this small street is inconsequential,
>
> Julia, worked at testing cultures and the stingy
>
> task, in every way irredeemable, of saving money

Then Allan came, his mother, left, came ill
squeezing a sewing machine into a hallway
and then the baby. Already you can see how
joylessness took a hold pretending to be joy

The economy or "forced economics" of living a life is revealed in line after line of the poem. Its underlying structure then recalls and calibrates the viciousness of modernity and late modernity as unfortunately the sound track of our lives—we are all moving. The poem *Thirsty* builds its poetics out of the tragedy of the police shooting of a Black man in the late 1970s; it appears to be Albert Johnson, a Black man living with mental health issues killed by the police in Toronto in 1976, the incident a watershed in Black organizing in the city. Brand, however, does not vindicate, instead she offers a reading of the city in which our entanglements of pain and beauty might signal one response to the traumas of the place. Brand thus writes of Toronto in the poem that it is a "city that had never happened before," a condition faced by many metropolitan cities long considering themselves in a post-1492 world as white or Euro-American cityscapes. *Thirsty* is a poem very local in its articulations, a kind of eulogy to Toronto, but much wider in its impact and its call to an ethics of living together in a community of which we might demand a ethico-politicality in its accord with a Derridean hospitality to the stranger.

In an earlier volume, *Land to Light On*, Brand is more pensive about the city. *Land to Light On* might be read at first as a disappointment in and refusal of the nation-state as a place of ethical belonging. In the poems the poet gives up on land to light on declaring, "I don't want no fucking country, here, there or all the way back." The poet moves to the hyper-immigrant local of Toronto to call nation and world into question and to demand an ethical accounting of the pain of contemporary movement. Thus, *Land to Light On* is a volume dedicated to making sense of how movement facilitates a particular kind of politics. In the poem "IV viii" (p.32) to "IV ix" (p.33) Brand turns the light back on the scholar, technological progress and liberal democracy. The poet will give each "Hutu/Tutsi a homepage" (p.32) and the "expert can no longer reach for anything" (p.33). Brand's critique of our intellectual stalemate does the work necessary to begin to think what renewal might be or look like.

In essays and short stories by Brand, the same kind of attention is paid to the politics of knowledge as the locus from which to view and engage a larger politics concerned with the international ethico-political. Anyone who is familiar with Toronto as a space and a place would not be surprised that one of Canada's best living poets would find in Toronto such inspiration (for lack of a better word). We want to turn to Brand's *What We All Long For* (2005). The novel writes the city of Toronto as it has never been written before, and it maps both city places and spaces, and the people like a cartographer's poetics denuded of its scientific claims. The novel monumentalizes Toronto through the ordinary and the everyday, with lives being lived in the small gestures of what it means to be human. Because Brand works with a notion that the city has never happened before, almost like Antonio Rojo's "the repeating island," her narrativizing of the city is in keeping with the Derridean notion of a "to come" possibility—the city is not finished, it never is. Brand's novel is in a fact a counterpoint to the neo-conservative and neoliberal desire to have the idea of multiculturalism disappear in favour of a consumer multiculturalism that allows for more flexible state management. *What We All Long For* is the story of such a refusal, along with the insistence of living a multiculturalism from below as the very basis of late modern life.

The characters in the novel are a group of twenty-something young people of colour, for whom the history of colonial/modernity gives us their designation, their categorization as particular genres of the human. It is not a designation they seek to live up to, but it is one that frames them and their actions nonetheless. They are either migrant to the city at a very young age or born of first generation migrant parents, for whom their children's cultural difference is both shared and confusing. But this is not a novel about generational conflict. This is a novel about migrant subjectivity even when there is no place to return to, as is the case for those born of the category immigrant parents and after. Instead, it is a novel about how cultural difference is lived as an excitement both crafted by us and simultaneously outside our reach. Brand neither celebrates nor denounces the idea of multiculturalism; she writes it and its possibilities, along with its outcomes. One of its outcomes is a creole sensibility or condition with all of the vicious pleasures that such entails.

Let us focus on one strand of the novel. The book concerns itself with all the various reasons that migration happens. One of the central elements concerns the character of Quy who is the brother of Tuyen, a young aspiring artist. Quy is separated from his family when they flee Vietnam in the 1970s. On that day, Quy does not hold on to his mother's hand tightly enough, and she loses him in the darkness of the night as the refugees run to board the boats of their smugglers. He eventually travels to Thailand where he becomes a part of the Thai underworld, later making his way to Toronto. Quy's mother is inconsolable in her loss, and his sister Tuyen wishes for his return so that she might be given the space she needs for self-expression in a family that has strict ideas for its youngest girl-child. Tuyen is neither Vietnamese nor Canadian, she is her very own local self—a self marked more by the ambient rhythms of the urban, than by any national geography, mythology or appeals to specific cultural claim.

As for Quy, for much of his life he is stateless. In fact, Quy's character calls to mind certain aspects of Agamben's insights on the place of law and no-law. Quy is the kind of refugee who sits in a wasteland and is indeed waste, existing outside state laws yet contained by state laws concerning movement, but for which no law can speak on his behalf. This place of law without law is one technology of the colonial/modern that is both continuous with the early colonial period and discontinuous with it in terms of the technologies of global juridical orders. Because Agamben can't seem to get to racial and plantation slavery in his rules of exception this theory remains inchoate for thinking these moments adequately. Nonetheless, Quy's total existence from the night he was lost has been to survive below the radar of state organized human life while simultaneously being produced by it in a kind of niggerdom experience.

Through a series of events, Tuyen discovers Quy's existence in the city. She approaches him and arranges for him to meet his now estranged family. While waiting outside his family's home for Tuyen to prepare them for his entry back into their lives, Quy is shot in an apparent carjacking. Quy's apparent death at the hands of a stranger to him, but not to his sister Tuyen, is one of the moments in the novel where the politics of late modernity's violence and crime in its complicated and internecine forms announces its most brutal reality. Brand's writing of this violent rupture of potential familial reconciliation is, we would suggest, the task that we have not been capable of attending to in the Humanities and Social Sciences; that is, what forms of knowledge, beyond the management of the disciplines, we require to stem the violences of our more intimate living in a post-World War Two hyper-migrant world.

The tragic circumstances of Quy's apparent death act as at least one of the conditions through which new knowledges, new ways of being and new relations will have to be found in the aftermath. There is no single aspect of Brand's novel that makes it utter the deep textures of Toronto's creole sensibility and form. Rather the textures of the novel, both thick and thin, pervade the work and in its most hopefully ethnographic sense give the reader an idea of what pervades that landscape and the possibilities to come. It is in this sense that creolization is a process towards what Sylvia Wynter calls "new forms of human life." How then might scholars think these new forms of life to come?

Interestingly as well, Austin Clarke has chronicled the space of Toronto over many years. From the Toronto Trilogy to *In This City* to *More*, he has written the underside of immigrant disappointment, a lying nostalgia for home and a certain kind of resentment and yet humorous appreciation of the irrationalities of this world. We want to focus briefly on *More*, because it highlights the problem of post-World War Two migrations. What does Black non-freedom look like after the war for "human rights"?

In *More*, Clarke gives us a wholly unreliable protagonist and a wholly unreliable narrator as well—sometimes merging both character and narrator. *More* launches a critique at logic and rationality while still revealing truths. Clarke's intention seems to throw back at us in searing madness the continuing violence of the Enlightenment project, only as it is interrupted by swathes of desires for a post-World War Two freedom that is never achieved. Idora might be living in a post-slavery world, but her emancipation, her freedom is very much in doubt, although not under conditions recognizable as plantation slavery. These are indeed new temporal conditions and new arrangements of being non-human Black.

Idora, the unbelievable protagonist, rails against injustice in the world and injuries inflicted and still being felt across history into the present. But her logic of life, time and morality does not allow us to simply read her pain as a continuation of slavery. Instead, we must understand Idora as embodying all of the contradictions of a post-Enlightenment society, one in which morality is situational (she asked her son to help her steal but is aghast that he might be a gangster) and where racism still operates just below the surface of the skin, but is nonetheless operational enough for cops to imagine Black boys as ants. Idora, who is herself not a very likeable character/person, offers readers reflections on injustice, raising both moral and ethical issues for our consideration. Idora articulates a global critique of racism and raciological thinking, moving from the USA to England to France to Holland and then to Montreal and closer to home in Toronto. Her critique of Canadian multiculturalism encapsulates and spits out its problem as one of modern segregation.

> "Multiculturalism? Is multiculturalism, you say? What is so multicul-
> turalistic about Toronto? Toronto is a collection of ghettos. Ethnic
> ghettos. Cultural ghettos. In other words, racial ghettos, and—" (p.256).

Idora proceeds to list all the ethnic ghettos in Toronto from Rosedale to "Jane-Finch: black people and visible minorities," (p.257) to Woodbridge and in-between. Her critique announces what rapper Jelleestone designates, as "the hood is here" for the working poor and racialized. Idora uses a broader brush; she refuses to be relegated to the category of the multicultural, or the visible minority and instead is intent on pointing out how we are all caught up in this deeply dissatisfying thing. She refuses to engage the celebratory decoration going under the anemic moniker of "historically ethnic neighbourhoods" to remind, maybe even call to attention European modernity's practices of categorization still so evidently with us and its debilitating force for BlackLife.

When Idora's critique turns to her son BJ—now Rashan Rashanan, a convert to Islam and a seeming gangster, the contradiction of a post-World War Two epistemology reveals itself. Idora is both all about racial solidarity and not. She rails against "African names" and wonders why young Black women and boys, like her son, are refusing the sweet and good Anglo names their parents gave them. At the same time, she can both dreamily imitate and admire the Muslim women in their headscarves and hijab as they walk by her basement window for the beauty of their dress. What Idora allows us to see is how the realities of Black crime, criminality and death force the question of the discontinuity between the immediate freedom of the temporal post-slavery world and the production of freedom in a post-civil rights, global migratory world and its resulting disappointments. Both Idora and BJ/Rashan are subjected to and subject to, as well as subordinated by, the "hidden" narratives of modernity's inherent history of violence and its continuity.

BJ/Rashan is the equivalent of Kardinal's Freshie, with whom we began. But in BJ/Rashan's troubles Clarke offers us an eye to the global wasted. In Moss Park, where the Armoury was built for the Second World War, all of those populations considered waste congregate: the homeless, drug dealers, prostitutes, alcoholics, the poor and disabled—the list and the categories are endless. It is indeed this light that Clarke flashes on our moment that allows us to pay witness to violence as more than gun crime and to see in gun crime the violent ordering of a world and globe through the partial perspective of the internalization of the contradictory and disciplinary mechanisms of a post-1492 perspective of the globe.

HERE AT HOME IN THE WORLD: RETURNING TO THE NARROWLY SOCIAL?

In short, Brand and Clarke rebuke and rewrite the violence and indeed the crimes of European modernity past and present. As artists they do not get us outside of violence; they highlight, though, the small and mundane moves by which it captures and secures its hold on us. Our task as scholars, along with the artists, is to begin to figure a way out of it. In the last decade, Canada has been repeatedly rated as one of the top ten western countries in which to reside. But persistent poverty amongst Black and Indigenous peoples in Canada tells a different story of the top rating. Significantly, violence and crime turned and focussed inward constitutes one of the most severe late modern practices of our time in the midst of much abundance and wealth.

As Hall *et al, In Policing the Crisis* point out, in such cases social control and authoritarian measures become at least one way to blunt the force of such capitalist contradictions, alongside programs of moral regulation. In this regard, the racialized poor find themselves the victims of a vulgar and old colonialism alongside a new colonial paradigm in which race and class collapse into each other. In effect, one can almost predict class status based on how one is racialized. Central to this new dynamic is what we call the cultural arm of neoliberalism, in which moral regulation, guilt and self-blame come to constitute the rationale for the wasted populations with those populations blaming themselves for the injustice done to them. In this context, the state becomes the arbiter of brutalizing and unequal power across a range of institutions. These institutions must produce modes of knowing or knowledges that support the continuing justification of wasted human lives and possibilities—what we might call the sagging pant syndrome. These conditions are best apprehended in the moment that characterizes Black poor youth's excision from the body politic. What Hall *et al* call the "social history of social reaction" is crucial to the policing of Black youth here. They write:

> Schematically, it begins with the unresolved ambiguities and contradictions of affluence...It is experienced first, as a diffused social unease, as an unnaturally accelerated pace of social change, an unhingeing (sic) of stable patterns, moral points of reference. It manifests itself... as an unlocated surge of social anxiety...on the hedonistic culture of youth, on the disappearance of the traditional insignia of class...Later, it appears to focus on more tangible targets: specifically, on the anti-social nature of youth movements, on the threat to British life by the black immigrant, and on the 'rising fever chart' of crime (p.321).

Black poor youth in contemporary North America and the West highlight the analysis of Hall *et al.* The moral panic concerning street crime, as opposed to the ethics of making a life livable, has brought to the fore the ways in which migration as both a reality and a dominant element of modernity continues to be a force to reckon with. Taken together Black poor and working poor youth, as disposal populations, force us in a number of different ways to account for the exclusive machinations of modern nation-state citizenship.

The response to this complicated and contradictory story of modern disappointment is Michel Foucault writing of the classical carceral age where he makes an argument that seems wholly applicable to our time. He writes: "A subtle, graduated carceral net, with compact institutions, but also separate and diffused methods, assumed responsibility for the arbitrary, widespread, badly integrated confinement of the classical age" (p.297). Earlier Foucault tells us that the prison becomes the site where classical practices of condemnation are solidified, reinstating many practices that the French Revolution has sought to abandon and diffusing them "across a great carceral continuum that diffused penitentiary norms into the very heart of the penal system and placing over the slightest illegality, the smallest irregularity, deviation or anomaly, the threat of delinquency" (p.297). As a theorist of one aspect of European modernity, Foucault's insights on the birth of the prison and its pervasive effects are both useful and simultaneously troubling for our analysis. His prison never meets the plantation and the other conditions that make prisons logical modes of regulation.

CONCLUSION: GLOBAL PENAL STATE

Michel Foucault's unmasking of the functioning and disciplinary use of the understanding of the work of various categories as one of power, the juridical and conduct—was incapable of, or refused to see how the history of slavery bears down on the diffusing of mechanisms and technologies of punishment in his *Discipline and Punish: The Birth of the Prison*. While slavery eluded Foucault's analysis as a scholar, its practices haunt each page of *Discipline and Punish*. That we might read the plantation as a technology of the modern, in which the practices of power, its internalized disciplinary modes, its internalized dynamics of conduct of the self and a perverted juridical and scientization become evident and are indeed the foundations of the modern and late modern penal state is not lost on anyone interested in Black global cultures.

James Baldwin, who walked, drank, smoked and maybe even partied in some of the same circles in Paris as Foucault, understood the profound consequences of the penal state for Black people in the USA (but one could now easily say globally). And while Foucault's "convict-ship" (p.299) never does meet the slave ship both he and Baldwin provide us with means to read how wasted human life is produced. In *The Fire Next Time*, Baldwin wrote

> And I know, which is much worse, and this is the crime of which I accuse my country and my countrymen, and for which neither I nor time nor history will ever forgive them, that they have destroyed and are destroying hundreds of thousands of lives and do not know it and do not want to know it (p.5).

Baldwin's writing, with its prophetic qualities, continually gestures to the penal state of the USA writ both large and small. The prison industrial complex is the contemporary site for the production of the conditions of Black poor degradation across numerous liberal democratic nations in which forms of global niggerdom or the NHI are continually produced. The crisis of incarcerated Black people in North America that the artists we have discussed above point toward allows us to glance at the new modes of thought that might dismantle the classificatory systems that produce global niggerdom.

The brilliance of Nas's album lies in the ways in which the penal state haunts almost every track on the album. On the last track "Black President" Nas quite pointedly asks of the then President-elect Barack Obama:

> we in need of a break
> I'm thinkin' I can trust this brotha
> But will he keep it real?
> Every innocent n!gger in jail—gets out on appeal
> When he wins – will he really care still?
> I feel...

Now we all know, if we care to notice, that the prison industrial complex has wreaked havoc on the Black family, and interestingly it has almost never been a significant point of debate in recent US presidential and congressional elections. Except for one hint in Obama's (2008) "A More Perfect Union" speech, he himself does not address the dire effects of what has now been termed the "new Jim Crow." The constant law and order issues of contemporary western societies characterized by the surveillance, security and fear state have built on the slave ship and the plantation into a trajectory of mass control.

In those homo-social places called prisons the perversity of the Americas now takes root and this is not just in the US. Prisons have become the late modern "plantations," in which a new chapter of BlackLife is being produced and simultaneously disposed. The complexity of the situation cannot be lost on those of us asked to think blackness and its value as an essential element of the labour we do. In our view, the grotesque condition of the prison industrial complex is at least one ground zero among many (BlackLife too causes ground zero to proliferate as a metaphor and an idea), in which the violence and crime of late modernity makes itself present and felt. The late Lindon Barrett, in his analysis of the complexities and complications of the field of inquiry where actual Black bodies must and do meet their scholarly inventions, makes use of the grotesque to call attention to the complications of the Black body in scholarship and beyond.

> Insofar as the grotesque is necessarily the African American body, it cannot, without some measure of disturbance, be thought in the U.S. landscape and cannot, without very great disturbance, be taken as of value or significance. Such speculative possibilities are most often, as a matter of course, determined speculative impossibilities. Interests in

the "never individual" life and "interstitial" nonidentity of "grotesque" black bodies never easily enters U.S. culture, or U.S. contemplative thought, of any period (p.144).

The question of value is indeed one that we must now urgently grapple with. Taking risks, making new knowledge and speaking truths as opposed to seeking truths are the tasks ahead of us if we might at the least interrupt the viciousness of modernity's classificatory systems and their always deferred promises. As Wynter reminds us, we scholars/artists/intellectuals are a central element of the classificatory system where "young black males can be perceived, and therefore behaved towards, only as the *lack* of the human, the *conceptual* other of North America" (p.13). She concludes by telling us: "They are the truth. It is we who institute this "truth". We must now undo their narratively condemned status" (p.16).

2

Black Gifts, Black People: 'Lament for a Nation' and Reading Canada in the Americas

Marx remains an immigrant chez nous, a glorious, sacred, accursed but still a clandestine immigrant as he was all his life. He belongs to a time of disjunction, to that "time out of joint" in which is inaugurated, laboriously, painfully, tragically, a new thinking of borders, a new experience of the house, the home, and the economy. Between earth and sky. *One should not rush to make of the clandestine immigrant an illegal alien or, what always risks coming down to the same thing, to domesticate him* (Jacques Derrida, *Specters of Marx*, p. 174, emphasis added).

Perceiving the lost subjects of history—the missing and lost ones and the blind fields they inhabit—makes all the difference to any project trying to find the address of the present. And it is the writing of the history of the present that is, I think, the sociologist's special province (Avery Gordon, *Ghostly Matters* p.195).

There is a sense in the mind of not being here or there, of no way out or in. As if the door had set up its own reflection. Caught between the two we live in the Diaspora, in the sea between. Imagining our ancestors stepping through these portals one senses people stepping out into nothing: one senses a surreal space, an inexplicable space. One imagines people so stunned by their circumstances, so heartbroken as to refuse reality. Our inheritance in the Diaspora is to live in this inexplicable space. That space is the measure of our ancestors' step through the door toward the ship. One is caught in the few feet in between. The frame of the doorway is the only space of existence (Dionne Brand, *A Map to the Door of No Return*, p.20).

I want to draw a map, so to speak, of a critical geography and use that map to open as much space for discovery, intellectual adventure, and close exploration as did the original charting of the New World—without the mandate for conquest (Toni Morrison, *Playing in the Dark*, p. 3).

A society or nation such as Canada, founded on the principles of white supremacy and racism, cannot ever succeed in developing a society free of the injustices that spring from these systems of thought, without a clearly articulated policy on the need to eradicate these beliefs (M. NourbeSe Philip, "Why Multiculturalism Can't End Racism", p.185).

We are bored with Canada. We are bored with the ongoing attempts to make Canada right. We are bored with scholarly and intellectual exercises meant to bring nuance to the violences that institute Canada as a formation. We are bored with the crime that Canada is and represents. But yet, we keep returning to a particular scene of the crime. The crime is the founding of the nation-state we now call Canada. The scene in question is that of how Black people and blackness is revealed and simultaneously erased in the unfolding violent drama called contemporary Canada. We keep returning to the scene of the crime because in our contemporary conversations the multiple forms of collusion structuring how Black people show up threatens to both undo and remake what might be at stake in the world that is increasingly more de-territorialized at the same time as all around the world Indigenous peoples' "resurgence" has turned our attention to land, as both territory and something more. We return to the scene of the crime because we have come to believe that these debates hold a crucial and difficult set of concerns for Black peoples in the Americas, especially those who are the descendants of the formerly enslaved.

The claims we will make about contemporary Canada must in fact be read as an antagonism with some discourses of the nation-state, land, decolonization and freedom as those ideas produce modes of anti-blackness, especially in the territory we call Canada, that continue to produce Black people and blackness as outside the terms of a present and future in which we might exist as more than a post-Enlightenment, late capitalist alibi for rescue. By this we mean what is now being proffered as decolonization still appears to imagine Black peoples as out of place, as a problem to be solved, as a spectre lurking in the midst of a problem that might otherwise be more readily solved. To state such is to notice the ways in which multiple forms of collusion now unfold, ready to shore up a version of the nation-state, a so-called reconciling nation-state, in which Black people remain a troubling addendum to others' freedom since our unfreedom cannot be unseen, even if it is not commented on nor acknowledged as fundamental and foundational to that which whiteness and its adjuncts now falsely claims it wants to reconcile with.

Therefore, in this chapter we turn to the haunt of history, and its Black ghosts, while at the same time attempting to think what Canada means as one node in the post-Columbus Americas. To do this work we turn to the archive and to an archive of Black gifts as a way to make sense of both our boredom and the ongoing repeating discovery of Black Canada as a surprise, eschewing what Sylvia Wynter (1995) would call wonder. How Black Canada appears, and/or is asked to appear never seems to do much to the archive of Canada. Indeed, Black Canada's repeated appearance seems more routine indifference than any genuine attempt to shift what Canada might mean, and yet we keep at it. As the philosopher Jacques Derrida points out, the archive is "spectral." But most importantly, "[t]he archivist produces more archive, and that is why the archive is never closed. It opens out of the future." Derrida continues: "But it is the future that is at issue here, and the archive as an irreducible experience of the future" (p.68). These ideas about the archive as both living and the future inform the ways in which we return to the historical as an opening up of both the present and the past in an attempt to make the present and the past touch the future.

In contemporary Canadian (literary, cultural, social and political) Studies blackness is not just relegated to the past, it still is almost non-existent. By this we mean that when blackness appears in Canadian (literary, cultural, social and political) Studies it is rarely understood as a constitutive element of what it means to be a Canadian despite decades of scholarship demonstrating otherwise. We wonder what causes this blockage? We are curious about what is at stake that Black people and blackness continue to occupy the site of surprise rather than wonder. This conundrum is crucial to understanding why the normative, ongoing story of Black people in Canada is a history of their relative recentness to Canada despite evidence to the contrary. To account for Black people as constitutive to the earliest formation of the nation would render the normative myth of two founding peoples suspect immediately. To render the narrative of the founding of the nation suspect would be to open up the origins of violence at the very foundation of the founding of the nation. And yet, the discourse of Canada as a benevolent nation means that blackness is not denied, but it is importantly not positioned as instrumental to national meaning either. It is the task of this chapter to query what might happen if blackness was and is assumed as instrumental to the formation of the nation and concurrently understood as a gift to both the past and the present, animating a different coming future.

NOT A BLACK LAMENT FOR THE NATION

While we in no way intend to characterize all Black history within the nation as one of a migrant or migratory nature—migration is central to all Black histories, especially those in the Americas. This is so, because the central forced migration—transatlantic slavery—resulted in an enormous Black density across the range of the Americas, from North to South, and more recently elsewhere as well. The story or rather impression of migration that we want to tell is not a new one, but we want to try to give it a different valence, tone, rhythm or to place another impression on it. In effect, all of us might become native to a place we did not originally belong to, to paraphrase Jamaica Kincaid. Taking Kincaid seriously, we might be able to achieve a different story of Canada. A story that allows for making reparations with the violent founding acts of early nation-state formation in which BlackLife still appears in jeopardy and precarious.

Blackness in contemporary Canada is, despite having Black populations of many generations, continually forced to announce itself as belonging and repeatedly claiming and refusing new-ness here. Such a gesture, such a suggestion, makes the continuous story of a Black presence that precedes post-World War Two migrations absent from popular imaginations of all Canadians—including some Black ones. We are intellectually exhausted by the repetition to make BlackLife worthy, to have it noticed, to have it studied as more than an example, as more than a product in service of something else (McKittrick, 2017). We are exhausted by continually having to refuse the multiple ways in which practices of Black subordination come to be in Canada's institutions. We now wonder if Canadian (literary, cultural, social and political) Studies can ever really find a way to engage blackness that is a sustained conversation, a peer at the table, one in which Black intellectual history and thought is continuous, impactful, and necessary to all of us beyond the immediate affect of surprise.

In George Grant's (1965) *Lament for a Nation: The Defeat of Canadian Nationalism* he trades in the continued lie, or to be more generous, the myth of the "two original peoples" who founded Canada. These two peoples in Grant's nationalist and ethnocentric fears he termed "French and Catholic, British and Protestant, united precariously in their desire not to be a part of the great Republic; but their reasons were quite different" (p.40). One could read Grant's comment here as a kind of collusion— a collusion that works against all the others. While Grant is defending Canadian-ness *vis a vis* disdain for the US and its mid-twentieth century empire, his defence—his lament—consecrates the myth of the founding of the nation as one that is both ordained in a certain way as English and French and also destined to be so. The logic of Grant's claim is to place all those outside the category of (white) English and French as adjuncts to the nation. Multiculturalism later formalizes these adjuncts into communities, allowing for some to enter whiteness against the block of non-white others.

Now, of course Grant is also writing against the USA. And it would not be too trivial to suggest that blackness bears down heavily on what is at stake for him, even when he does not directly address blackness. At the time of Grant's writing the civil rights movement is at its peak and the spectre of blackness haunts his text in all kinds of ways. Thus we might also read Grant's fear of the US as too steeped in the fear of how blackness there occupies a contestatory space vis a vis whiteness and its own claims of national founding. One significant way that Grant's lament works is to also rhetorically deny blackness historical space in Canada. This denial that is endemic to Grant's text runs across the works of Canadian white male philosophers like Harold Innis and Marshall McLuhan too.

A Canada that cannot or refuses to conceptualize its relation to transatlantic slavery and its formation, as a part of the post-Columbus slave-world is a Canada that will continually have difficulty with Black people. This argument goes beyond making the evidence of slavery in Canada appear and be present and a part of our conversation, to also suggest that Canada's own place in the Atlantic world is imbued with slave logics; the evidence of slavery's existence here is but only one part of a larger history, dynamic and consciousness. We think, for example, of Canada's historic trade in salted cod used to feed those enslaved in the Anglo-Caribbean as one example of the suppression of Canada's deep imbrication in the Atlantic world of slavery, its practices, its economies, its ideologies and its logics. Indeed, Grant and Innis, in particular, in their attempts to produce a political philosophy that centres Canada as a nation-state have both failed, one might argue, or deliberately decided to engage Canada's place in the slave-holding Atlantic world as central to its founding and thus its ongoing existence.

The myth of two original peoples then allows for others to be imagined in the nation as always recent, as always having just arrived, just migrated. And it simultaneously allows white settlers to claim a natural belonging and to have a history of arrival at the same time. Indeed, to inhabit a history of arrival and to offer reconciliation is a masterful political move. In that move a new compact is being created; it is a compact that asks Indigenous peoples to enter Canada. In my (Walcott's) previous work on the question I have argued not only does it ask Indigenous peoples to enter Canada, but also to enter a Canada that was founded to always already exclude them. But if I might be so bold, reconciliation is not much different from Bartolomé de las Casas in his decree that Indigenous peoples had a soul and therefore should not be enslaved, but Africans were fair game for the brutal subjugations of mining and plantation slavery. Reconciliation, then, still demands an Indigenous less-than-human-self that might be rescued, but it is a self nonetheless. Black selfhood remains in this moment still outside the category of European Man. In this moment the question is one of how national institutionality responds to reconciliation from multiple sites of guilt, privilege and power to exactly state what reconciliation looks like. And, we should be clear that reconciliation is not transformation, remaking and decolonization.

Flowing from this, Canadian (literary, cultural, social and political) Studies' liberal multicultural approaches to Black Canada remain steeped in (anti-)blackness as only constituting the example to and for something else. In real terms, then, Black people and their gifts are still commodified in service of producing whiteness and white people in an unbroken relation to slavery (with their adjuncts now sometimes more included). How many of you are working to institute forms of Black knowledges and their production, meaning Black thinkers, into your various institutions? How might it be in this moment of white reconciliation that white people, especially white scholars, speak a "we of settlers," meant to enfold Black people in that plurality? How is the thought, the idea, even possible, if Grant's thinking is still not in some way underwriting what Canada is and means? And if Black people's enslavement remains out of the purview of the definition of colonization being used? We pose these as dead serious questions because in this moment of reconciliation, white desires, demands, and order of knowledge continue to proliferate. We pose these as questions seeking to ask how might Black knowledges show up as more than possessions for white performative identity making? We pose these as questions because we see continually who moves across our institutions, who matters to them, who gets the call for the interview, who gets the job. We are exhausted by Canadian (literary, cultural, social and political) Studies anti-blackness posing as engagement with Black people and their expressive cultures. One might make the analogy between the use of Black literary products and knowledges as not unlike the historic trade in salted fish and rum. White folks profit, once sugar is king, until no longer needed; bounty then, now obsolete. And in that process from profit to obsolescence the story of Black people's relation to the formation of Canada goes missing. We are exhausted by a Canadian (literary, cultural, social and political) Studies that prefers Black products minus Black people; as Dionne Brand states, "Our inheritance in the Diaspora is to live in this inexplicable space" (p.20). Such an inexplicable space is one in which Black people get folded into the category of settler by white people and some Indigenous people, but never do Black people get others to account for the theft of our subjectivity as the enslaved in the Americas. How do you reconcile that?

BLACK GIFTS AS A PROBLEM

In this section, we turn to what we will call three Black gifts: the Sir George Williams Affair, Africville and Caribana. We argue that these are gifts that allow for a range of relations to nation, citizenship, belonging and anti-Black institutionality that might allow for thinking differently about what is at stake in terms of thinking Canada in the Americas. These three gifts require that we think in sustained ways about Black events that refashion this nation. The ongoing salted cod cultural politics of cultural analysis, institutions and practitioners consistently means that Black cultural workers write the same essay over and over again. We have written this document before; it is why we are exhausted. So, let us turn yet again to repeating and recounting that which should by now be shaping all of our conversations about this place, this nation, this land, but still resolutely does not.

The Sir George Williams Affair encapsulates Walcott's claim for a diasporic reading that places Canada in the Americas. The Affair concerned itself with students bringing a complaint against a biology professor, Perry Anderson, at the end of the term in April 1968 for discriminatory grading practices at George Williams University. The administration dragged its feet on the complaint hoping it would disappear by the beginning of a new term in the autumn of 1969. This was a bad calculation on the administration's part. However, over the course of that period two important events had taken place in Montreal. The first event was the Congress of Black Writers held in October 1968, which also travelled to Toronto in a reduced fashion and with some different speakers. Among the speakers at the conference were: C. L. R. James, Stokely Carmichael and James Forman, Harry Edwards, Walter Rodney, Bobby Hill, Alvin Poussaint, Rocky Jones, Michael X, Lloyd Best and Jan Carew. Eldridge Cleaver and Amiri Baraka were denied entry into Canada to participate as was planned. Additionally, the Hemispheric Conference to End the War in Vietnam also occurred that November with participation from Bobby Seale and a number of notable Third World radicals (Roberts, 2005). It was in the context of such intellectual and activist engagements, including other conferences that ran from 1965 until 1969, that the Affair eventually unfolded. These events meant that Black people had and were making the links for justice in Canada with similar struggles elsewhere—they were not just imitating or voicing support for struggles elsewhere. They understood their plight as one characterized by global forces, but especially the historical forces of the Americas.

The main event of the Affair was the taking of the Computer Centre and its occupation by a number of students (400 of them) for two weeks at the end of January and into February in 1969. The occupation culminated in a fire and the police storming the Centre on February 11. Significant damage was reportedly done to some of the computers, apparently about two million dollars worth; this resulted in a bevy of charges being laid against the students involved. The outcome of the occupation, not unlike other student occupations that occurred at that time throughout the western world, was broken up by severe police brutality; a university administration that was unrepentant in its call for the authorities to act; a judicial system that authorized and supported stringent punishment (bail ranged from $1,000 to $15,000); and a society that by and large refused to acknowledge the legitimacy of the students' complaints (Eber, 1969; Forsythe, 1971). And yet, the situation was also much more complex than our last sentence suggests.

It was not only Black students who occupied the Computer Centre; white student allies and others did as well. Additionally, former students like Alfie Roberts, an intellectual and community organizer, were involved and offered more than support; and while in the aftermath of the police brutality and the ensuing trials the Black community of Montreal came together, initially the older Black community was somewhat reticent to support what they perceived as "unruly" Caribbean Blacks breaking a "racial contract" (Mills, 1997) that some of them felt had worked well enough for a long time. Significantly, a number of the students involved of Caribbean descent had no intention of living in Canada beyond university and thus were foreign students. They were intent on making the historical and contemporary links between racism and anticolonial struggles. All of these ingredients made the Sir George Williams Affair a far more significant event than it appears in Canadian Studies scholarship. We are suggesting its significance has been minimized, if not wholly ignored and even evaded in Canadian Studies and particularly in reassessments of the period.

Of the students involved in the Affair, two were eventually deported to the Caribbean and a third became a politician in Canada and sat in the Senate. Senator Anne Cools began as Liberal and Canada's first Black senator, but shifted her political allegiance to Conservative and then sat as an Independent when she became particularly active around the fathers' (men's) rights movement; she retired in August 2018. Roosevelt "Rosie" Douglas who was deported to Dominica after the Affair, eventually became the prime minister there in 2000, serving for eight months until his sudden death. In particular, we want to suggest by invoking those two figures that the Computer Centre occupation offers us the opportunity as scholars to recalibrate both history and the place of Black peoples in Canadian Studies. As Alfie Roberts (2005) suggests about the Black conferences and congresses held in Montreal in the 60s and the flare up at the Sir George Williams University Computer Centre: "I think it would be useful to say at this point that all of these congresses could be considered as a Black complement to the ongoing Quebecois Quiet Revolution" (p.73). The significance of these events can be tracked in what at the time might have been considered Canada's most radical Black newspaper, *Contrast*. The paper ran continuous stories on police brutality of Black people across Canada in the 60s and 70s and mobilized Black supporters of the students during and in the aftermath of the police invasion. *Contrast* was edited by Harold Hoyte the founder and publisher of one of the leading newspapers in Barbados today, established shortly after independence in the 70s; additionally, the now celebrated Black Canadian writer, the late Austin Clarke, was an editor in the 70s; and a number of Black Canadian journalists who eventually moved on to mainstream media in the late 1970s and 1980s got their start at the newspaper as well.

What we are suggesting is that the Sir George Williams Affair is more than a nationally bound event. But even in its extra-national qualities, it holds much for scholarship in Canadian Studies as the 60s and 70s uprisings become, and rightly so, canonized as initiating a new and more hopeful promise of human life, even if contemporary neoliberal forces have now achieved an abortion of many of those hopes. We are further suggesting that part of the task of Canadian Studies as a cross-disciplinary and interdisciplinary field is to engage these Black histories not merely as Black, but as centrally contributing to the formation of the modern nation-state of Canada and more, thus placing Canada firmly in the Americas and Atlantic slave culture, and even as state reformist practices like multiculturalism and now reconciliation. In short, Black action and resistance is a gift that shapes reform. Failure to do so on our part places both Black people and Black people's relationship with institutions like the university in a precarious position. By this we mean that the university, like policing, continues to exist as at least one disciplinary force among others for Black Canadians.

The much celebrated film *Ninth Floor* (2015, NFB) on the Sir George Williams Affair is a case in point. Mina Shum's rather problematic and deeply flawed film demonstrates the salted cod approach to Black cultural knowledge, texts, peoples and events. One might write about the director's excess of trivialities that add nothing to the story; or one might write about the ways in which the film's celebration is linked to intramural relations among friends that promote it as an important addition to Black expressive history when it is not; or one might raise the very difficult concern of what appears on celluloid as a lack of the director's knowledge of BlackLife; but to raise these concerns is not to sustain a conversation on what might be done when the intellectual apparatus of cultural criticism cannot sustain Black critique. What we want to point out here is that Black expression, in this case political action, is traded in service of the well being of a non-Black director and upheld by some Black actors committed to a particular liberal ideology of Canadian institutional multiculturalism. What is at stake is that a reversal with a Black director and an Asian Canadian story would most likely be untenable, never made. So, the question is what makes this possible? What makes it possible we must understand, is how the ongoing logics of transatlantic slavery continue to shape Canada's present relation to Black peoples. Such logics are the routinized unconscious of the white people and their adjunct Americas as constituting an ongoing anti-Black (un)consciousness and set of logics in which Black people remain commodities (Austin, 2013).

Two other events play a significant role in the argument we are attempting to make—the destruction of Africville and the gift of Caribana. Africville, Nova Scotia, one of Canada's oldest Black communities was finally and permanently razed to the ground in 1969. The demolition had begun at least two years prior when urban planners from the University of Toronto submitted a report to the Halifax city council justifying the council's desires to raze the community. Africville was indeed in bad shape. But Africville was also a close-knit community of many generations, which had been deliberately neglected by the city of Halifax, and for which the city had developed a new-found appetite for its land. We will not go into all the details of the Africville demolition, but we do want to stress a few points. 1. When Africville was demolished, a significant number of its residents moved down the eastern seaboard to the USA. 2. Many other residents were relocated to social housing in Uniacke Square, which has now emerged as one of Halifax's most notorious ghettos and is now again being gentrified, pushing Black people out. 3. The people in Africville owned their homes and took great pride in that knowledge. 4. The state outright refused to invest in urban renewal in Africville, in spite of residents' calls to so do over many years. 5. The university's implication in the violence of Africville and the struggle by the still-living residents of Africville and their descendants. Those of us interested in the relationship between knowledge and violence find it difficult to contemplate that stories and instances like Africville still occupy the place of the "special effect" in Canadian Studies. By that we mean we repeatedly tell these stories, again and again making little or no impact on the normative story that Odimumba Kwamdela's *Niggers This is Canada* (1971) has his immigrant voices on arrival refer to as "Good ol' Canada".

Two years prior, in Canada's centennial year, some of those same immigrants organized to give Canada the gift of Caribana. Caribana was only possible as a gift if seen within the context of Black global struggles and Black self-assertiveness in the face of both the anticolonial movements, specifically in this case from the Caribbean, and the shift of the civil rights movement from the language of integration to one of cultural autonomy as in Black Power. Stressing the global connections of these actions, it is important to note that around this time Caribbean-derived carnivals were founded in Britain and the US as well. The crucial moment here is that shortly after the gift was given and fairly well received the festival quickly plunged into troubles, all of which come to be associated with a blackness that is in some ways foreign to Canada. At the same time, over the now forty-year history of the festival its economic contribution has been difficult to deny. One of the desired goals for the founders of Caribana was to establish a Black community/cultural centre. The dream has not yet materialized. The dismal fate of Caribana's desires, we think, encapsulates the historical trajectory we have been plotting here—the inability of the nation to reconcile its Black populations as instrumental to its formation. Violence has been one of the main reasons that for almost thirty-eight years Caribana has struggled to be understood as a Canadian event. But we would resignify violence and redirect it at the state for its inability to render blackness a sustained element of Canadian-ness.

From where we stand Canadian (literary, cultural, social and political) Studies is deeply implicated in such violence. The idea that Black people remain marginal to the formation of Canada as a modern nation-state is one whose time should now be over—the end of George (the generic name given to Black sleeping car porters) so to speak. But what is clear about the uprisings of the 60s and 70s in Canada is that while a series of doors were opened for a range of different peoples, those same doors were being simultaneously shut for Black Canadians—both metaphorically and materially. The lack of any sustained studies or centres for the study of Black Canadian life means that the role of the university in perpetuating violence against Black people in multiple forms is crucial to understanding how Black people are placed and disciplined in Canada and its other national institutions.

While the 60s and 70s provided the framework for renewed conversations on questions of race in the USA and for achieving national independence for others, in the post-war period in Canada a different tack was taken. In Canada, while the racial tension diminished somewhat, what came into its place was a skilful selection of individual persons as representatives for the Black community in a newly re-imagined multicultural Canada; these persons' selection were never sustained, nor were they the route or the mechanism to serious avenues for advancement, so that others might have similar opportunities. Indeed, now in the early part of the new millennium the emergence of a Black underclass is a serious phenomenon that requires careful and thoughtful action in all of Canada's major cities.

CONCLUSION

And yet, a new gift is given. Black people give to save their lives, while whiteness and white people continually seek new modes of justification for ongoing colonial anti-Black practices that normalize their placement as legitimate anywhere whiteness shows up. In the era of Black Lives Matter, both as movement and organization, the Black gifts to Canada continue unabated. The year 2017 marked fifty years of Caribana, discussed above, a gift so entirely stolen from Black people that to invoke it is to also invoke the tears of anger. The three gifts above taken together constitute yet another moment when Black people in Canada might reanimate the violent founding of the nation within the Americas as one in which the foundational violences that animate our thought and our institutional routinizations work at the sites of a deep and abiding anti-blackness. At the level of institutional knowledge production of studies on Canada, the question of race remains urgent, and one might argue that if Canadian Studies does not seek to "understand the irrational-rational logic that has facilitated its survival" (Austin, p.183) then Canadian Studies simply remains in a master relation to Black people and their expressive cultures.

With such in mind, contemporary BlackLife in Canada sits permanently in the structure of haunting. Much of it might be characterized as concerned with the hauntological. That is because much of it is concerned with the politics of belonging and its opposite; much of it is haunted by what it does not yet know, cannot tell, is forced to invent and does not want to know. Black Canadian expressive culture is yet to fully tell its free story. As literary historian and editor Richard Almonte points out in his introduction to Thomas Smallwood's, *A Narrative of Thomas Smallwood*, a slave narrative written in Canada, the narrative is at the least ambivalent about the place of its writing and production. Almonte interprets Smallwood's accounts of Canada as "contradictory" and as "ambivalence towards Canada" (p.18), while at the same time Smallwood "proudly" claims Canada as home. Smallwood's ambivalence can thus be read as prefiguring many of the scripts of contemporary Black Canadian expressive culture's responses to the nation. The question of ambivalence can be accessed in a range of Black Canadian works from literature to music to drama to film. Cecil Foster's *A Place Called Heaven: The Meaning of Being Black in Canada*, was one of the most discussed books in the 1990s on the place of Black people and blackness in the Canadian nation-state. *A Place Called Heaven* was written from the scene of desire and disappointment of the African-Caribbean immigrant and Foster reports that the children of immigrants were under-achieving their parents. Such knowledge was difficult for immigrant parents to bear since one of the principal desires of migration is often articulated as a desire for children to live better lives than their parents—is this not shared across blacknesses—Muslimness, queerness, transness? Thus migration is often popularly understood as parental sacrifice in the service of a better life for the child. While the address of Foster's book is mainly from the point of view of the Black Caribbean Canadian immigrant, it is also about the place of first and second generation Black Canadians and thus its address is entirely ambivalent about what the place of the latter might be in Canada. Foster's book asks the question of whether Canada can be "a place called heaven" as the Thomas Smallwoods of the US slave population allegorized it. To pose the question is to assert the sense of ambivalence that Almonte reads in Smallwood's narrative and that I read in Foster's book some one hundred and forty-five years later. This time lag is deeply characteristic of Black peoples' relation to Canada; it is one of ambivalence that is both a collective desire for full liberation and simultaneously a state-imposed sanction whereby the state apparatus makes it difficult to fully belong. The rhetoric of multiculturalism is deeply implicated in this sleight of hand citizenship status.

In one of the quotations that begin this chapter, NourbeSe Philip joins contemporary activists in their calls for social justice in the face of enduring white supremacy and anti-blackness. BLM and the Movement for Black Lives embody three to four decades of Black feminist ideas, politics and insights. Their formation, constituted of queer, trans, persons living with disabilities, heterosexuals, all-sexuals and on and on—a range of identities invoked as necessary naming and simultaneously incidental to an imagined future—calls to mind a coming together to get work accomplished. As June Jordan (1992, *Fireweed Feminist Quarterly*) once put it, "we're going to be as specific as possible in that way. So that we atomize these humongous concepts, white and not white, or white and Black, or people of colour, and so on, and get very specific like that, then we go back to the big one again" (p.38). By invoking a list of "intersectional identities," BLM demonstrates how all those identities route us back to the big question of BlackLife in a much more comprehensive fashion. They bring us a little bit closer to what freedom might mean.

So what do we mean by freedom, then? For us, freedom marks a certain kind of sovereignty over the self in relation to collective and communal conditions. In the context of unfreedom, we can glimpse modes of unauthorized being as self-authored acts pointing to or authorizing a potential freedom to come. Here we are thinking of the ways in which Black people break "rules," authorizing for themselves new ways of being in the world. These ways of being are often violently interdicted. Freedom is the gap or space between breaking the law and the re-imposition of the law or its variant—that is violence. The law is violence in this conception we are offering. The law, then, always curtails freedom for Black personhood in the West. It is the BLM call, that "we will win" in the face of contemporary state institutional (especially universities') violences of all kinds that keeps open the possibility of a freedom yet to come. And we must thank the movement for Black lives for the future they are making appear right now.

3

After Black Lives Matter:
Black Death, Capitalism and Unfreedom

WHEN BLACK LIVES DO NOT MATTER

The cultural scene in Canada, especially its literary, social, political and cultural institutions, exhibits all the qualities of global anti-blackness that in this moment of *Black Lives Matter* we might notice if we so care to. We begin this chapter about the culture industries broadly construed, with the invoking of the ongoing murders of Black people in North America because we believe that such murders are neither mere coincidence nor are they about to come to an end anytime soon. Indeed, if any single thing characterizes contemporary BlackLife in Canada, it is the way in which Black lives seem not to matter at all, especially in the nation's major institutions—museums, art galleries, universities, government and so on. Indeed, if there ever was a time in the recent past that making such a claim would have been seen as entirely cynical or even wrong and out of place, that time has now passed.

Even the much vaunted and celebrated Canadian state policy of multiculturalism has not been able to stem the foundation and ongoing tide of anti-blackness in Canada. Everywhere you look, BlackLife is in dire straits in Canada. Whether we are looking at poverty, prisons, joblessness, underemployment, unemployment, housing, education—the list could go on—BlackLife is mostly stuck somewhere at the bottom of every marker, along with Indigenous peoples. What is particularly striking is that no level of government or any other major institution in the nation ever seems to find it necessary to speak directly to Black people about their collective well-being, and thus the pain that Black people are collectively living with and under remains mostly out of view to others.

We will therefore address the ways in which contemporary protests concerning the deaths of Black people in North America have cast new light on thinking about the ways in which capitalism and its multiple forms of unfreedom is the foundation of those deaths. Significantly, it is important to note that the history of political activism by Black Canadians has often focused on police shootings and other forms of police misconduct alongside cultural activism. Working with the long and sustained Black critique of capitalism by Black intellectuals, we suggest that Black death cannot be delinked from the ways in which cultural institutions operate. Here we argue that BlackLife is and will always be shaped by forms of inequality, given that current capitalist foundations are premised on the historical foundation of the exploitation of Black unfree labour and simultaneously the excision of BlackLife from institutions and institutional power in part derived from that very labour. In this essay we argue for new forms of collective belonging and ways of life beyond capitalist organization and late modern articulations of the human.

THE POLITICS OF COMPROMISE IS ANTI-BLACK

The history of Black collective pain and exclusion is a rather long one, but we will locate this new condition of it from the 1980s onward herein. Indeed, in 1971 the late Pierre Elliott Trudeau introduced his multicultural policy to the Canadian parliament stating clearly that it would not change the character of the nation as consisting of two founding peoples—English and French. In 1988, the then Prime Minister Brian Mulroney made multiculturalism an Act of the Canadian Charter of Rights and Freedoms, which is an Act of the Constitution. Between the move from Policy to Act, political and cultural organizing among and by Black people, along with many others, achieved significant gains that mostly bore fruit in the late 1980s and throughout the 1990s.

In the late 1980s and 1990s, activists' protests attempted to open up the possibilities for art-making by people of colour across a wide range of disciplines, and the results of this work cannot and should not be easily discounted in Canada. For example, in publishing a range of small presses and major presses began to publish the works of non-white Canadians, producing a robust list of writers working in the novel and poetry. Indeed, in a certain register the cultural work was quite successful, drawing on the discourse of multiculturalism both to contest representation and to produce forms of state and other kinds of recognition. In other registers, the work was also tremendously personally and collectively painful and difficult, and some individuals paid a significant personal and professional price for challenging the system as it was then (here we think of the writer NourbeSe Philip). The challenge to institutional power at that time still bears its scars today. The silence on NourbeSe Philip, one of Canada's best living poets, is a case in point. It appears that she has as yet not been forgiven for her significant critiques of numerous Canadian cultural institutions and their racist programming as well as their structural racist exclusion.

What is quite profound about the art activism of that period is that the activists understood the problem to be a problem of structure already. But in that moment, they understood the practice of exclusion and misrecognition to be structural and therefore fixable. I will return to structure later, but suffice to say now, it is extremely clear that the structure was indeed not fixable and only malleable. The malleability of the structure allowed for a whole new set of structures to emerge to manage and buttress the inclusion of people of colour into existing institutions. Those new institutional arrangements, going under the names and functions of equity offices and equity officers came with well-conceived and written policies bearing the same names and offices conceived, developed, and implemented by activists invited by the institutions to sit on committees to spearhead institutional change. In fact, many artists found themselves in the aftermath of such committee work drawn into institutions to implement and run such offices. However, in the aftermath of 1980s/90s art activism, it is pretty clear that equity offices, equity officers and the most fantastic equity policies do not and cannot change structures that are fundamentally anti-Black.

Andrea Fatona (2011) has documented this period of arts activism in Canada by concentrating on the Canada Council for the Arts (CC). The CCA is a national body that funds professional artists across a range of disciplines. Its main method of assessment is the peer-review or juried method. Fatona documents the period between 1989-1999, a period that we have already claimed was the most fertile period of non-white artists contestations of exclusion, their simultaneous piecemeal inclusion and a creative output that has since dwindled. In this work she interviews all of the major players, artists and professionals who worked inside the CCS, including its senior directors, in the transformation of the CCS's engagement with non-white artists. In her study, Fatona finds that Black artist-activists played a significant and leading role not only in organizing and challenging the institution, but also in leading and working with the institution to effect meaningful change. Indeed, meaningful change, if it could be called that, was fleeting and one might argue it was not achieved at all. In the aftermath of these heroic efforts, NourbeSe Philip's critique remains important still. She wrote: "Multiculturalism as we know it, has no answers for the problem of racism or white supremacy—unless it is combined with a clearly articulated policy of anti-racism, directed at rooting out the effects of racist and white supremacist thinking" (Philip, 1992:185 in Fatona, 119). Fatona writes that the CCA eventually acknowledged institutional racism, unlike other institutions (193), but such an acknowledgement did not and does not support a sustained level of engagement for Black artists across Canada. So why is this so?

Indeed, it is our contention that post-2000 what became clearer was the ways in which anti-blackness at the structural level has worked and works to make Black art and Black artmakers disappear and/or only occupy a tangential relation to national institutions. Importantly, there is nothing like a crisis to demonstrate the ways in which racial capitalism shapes BlackLife. The repeated crises of neoliberal economy, alongside the security and state surveillance post-9-11, made this clear to many if it was not clear before. Fatona (2011) writes: "The issue of racial hierarchies amongst people of colour was mentioned in relation to the First Advisory Committee for Racial Equality at the Canada Council for the Arts. The issue also arose in my conversations with Black artists regarding multi-racial activist formations in the communities" (190). Racial hierarches work to produce 'the Black' as "the dysslected" other as Sylvia Wynter terms it, meaning the furthest away from whiteness and thus the most impossible to incorporate structurally. However, our argument is that incorporation is fundamentally impossible for 'the

Black.' Furthermore, the conditions under which incorporation is understood are so deeply freighted with the detritus of racial capital and white supremacist logics that incorporation can and only does occur at the symbolic level leaving all other Black beings or Black life forms (Walcott, 2014) marked for poverty and death as a repetition of modern life.

The starkness of our claims are positioned alongside the accounting for how neoliberal changes in full effect produced an abundance of what Zymunt Bauman (2003) has termed wasted lives. When one takes such an insight to the artworld and its institutions—galleries, publishing houses, museums, festivals and so on, one can see how these practices and conditions are linked to larger phenomena like Black death. The unsustainability of the project of incorporation is revealed in the moment that what looks like change meets its demise in the time of economic claims or a crisis of economy. We make this case because one could see a significant change in the Canadian artworld at the time of art activism in the 80s and the 90s but once that long decade came to a close, the kinds of activities that had been previously present and made possible by activism disappeared in the 2000s. Why was it not sustained? The 2000s mark the full onslaught of the neoliberal project in Canada. Thus, part of the story is the way in which neoliberal reordering of the economics of the cultural sphere impacted how policies for equitably sharing resources were interrupted by logics of efficiencies, radical individualism, managerialism, audit culture and so on. However, when neoliberalism and anti-blackness combined, the impact on Black art and Black art makers produced a profound context of disappearance and, one might say, remade the landscape in a manner that now calls for renewed forms of activism.

The world of writing is a case in point. The same writers who made the move from the small presses to the larger national and international presses exist today as they did two decades ago: Austin Clarke, Dionne Brand, Lawrence Hill, Cecil Foster, André Alexis and so on. A few younger writers (Esi Edugyan, David Chariandy) have made it into the realm, but by and large Black writers remain locked out of significant forms of circulation and their work is most published by small, not well circulating presses. This inability to sustain ongoing incorporation in fact points to how fundamentally the structural underpinnings remain and are indeed anti-Black. Incorporation only works temporally and temporarily at the moment of contestation and confrontation, but left alone, its routinization reverts back to exclusion and diminution. It is our argument that the unsustainability of incorporation is not merely anti-Black, but that its anti-blackness is foundational to capitalism and its asymmetrical and disjunctive practices—what we call inequality.

RACIAL CAPITALISM CANNOT BE REFORMED

We might want to ask why these failures exist despite what one might characterize, if being generous, as good intentions of attempted social change? The reality is that the history of most contemporary anti-racism struggles has been fraught with the problem of attempting to repair or renovate a system that cannot be repaired. In fact, one might make the claim that if a politics of destruction is not central to contemporary political organizing and resistance then such actions find themselves in a repetitive cycle. That cycle will merely continually delay, to put it mildly, desires for freedom and liberation by compromise, interruption and the undermining of more radical actions through incorporation into late modern capital. The point we are making here is one that is not new, but has been articulated by Frantz Fanon, Sylvia Wynter and a host of intellectuals and scholars working in what we call the Black radical tradition.

The cultural industries are a particularly pernicious and difficult problem for racial capitalism. In the contemporary era, when culture is invoked it is so often taken to be simply within the realm of representation—that is often understood as presence and recognition minus labour and compensation. The question of labour is often suspended or not acknowledged at all because the myth of art as something special and deeply personal still pervades how we tend to relate to it. Seldom are we forced to think of art as a form of labour, as requiring much more than the personal to animate its contributions to cultural life. So, if in general consciousness art-labour remains ephemeral, then for Black art-makers this problem is significantly compounded if not altogether unacknowledged. Since Black people hold a problematic relation to capitalism in general, it is further compounded for Black cultural workers, we would argue.

In what follows, we are guided by Cedric Robinson's (1983/2000) insights in *Black Marxism*, to articulate an understanding of racial capitalism that underpins our contemporary moment and our logics of economy and aesthetics. By racial capital, we mean to signal the co-constitutive coupling of the history of unfree African labour (racial/African enslavement) and ongoing white supremacy and Eurocentrism as producing the conditions through which BlackLife is conditioned, experienced and made known. To account for racial capitalism as a significant and ongoing force we must acknowledge that transatlantic slavery is the foundation of modern capitalism, both in practice and in its ideas. Edward Said's (1994) *Culture and Imperialism* remains one of the most significant excavations of the relationship between racial slavery, imperialism and the emergence of the modern. However, W.E.B. Du Bois, Eric Williams, and Cedric Robinson have also contributed significantly to our understanding of the development of racial capitalism and how it underpins the world as we presently know it and experience it.

Our assertion of racial capitalism is meant to make the link between the "discredited" cultural knowledges and practices that constitute anti-blackness and the ways in which premature Black death are along the same continuum. The argument is that racial capitalism has embedded in it all the elements necessary for the comingling of economy and social and cultural death as well as physical death. From C. L. R. James' *The Black Jacobins* to Du Bois' *The Suppression of the Atlantic Slave Trade* and *Black Reconstruction* to Williams' *Capitalism and Slavery*, these founding texts of racial capitalism offer us an analysis of modern capital that is indivisible from white supremacist and Eurocentric logics of the post-Columbus world. It is our argument, then, that strategies of inclusion framed as multiculturalism, equity, social justice and so on cannot and do not work towards Black freedom and liberation but instead reentrench inequality and brutalities of all kinds. The last two decades have shown us that reforming the existing state does not ameliorate Black suffering, but instead works to uphold logics that already cast blackness aside, to put it mildly. What is at stake, then, is a radical accounting of the underpinnings of contemporary life and how those underpinnings require Black waste and disposability as their very calculable logics.

Fred Moten, analyzing both Douglass and Marx, has been an astute analyst of the historical and contemporary relationship between Black unfreedom, labour and capitalism. Pinpointing how slavery makes 'the Black' both commodity and labour, Moten argues that both capitalism and its critics, as in Marx, failed to account for the commodity that speaks. The inability to make such an accounting means that BlackLife remains perpetually unacknowledged as always complicating capital in ways that we have yet to fully grapple with beyond those of the Black radical tradition. Moten has argued that Black people are "labourers who were commodities before, as it were, the abstraction of labour power from their bodies and who continue to pass on this material heritage across the divide that separates slavery and "freedom." (6) To be clear, the enslaved is a commodity even before arrival in the Americas as labourer, and indeed, the enslaved is never ever just labourer. It was the hybrid condition of labourer and its excess that complicated our historical present. Indeed, to come to terms with it will require new forms of being together that neoliberalism prohibits us from thinking at this present time. Suffice it to say that we must now begin to imagine new modes of living lives that exceed capital as the foundational element of "human" organization. By making such a claim, we call modernist logics into dispute as well given that those logics underpin capital's brutal calculus that everywhere marks BlackLife for death, from the "ghettos" of North America to the Strait of Gibraltar.

So, let us return, then, to the deadly outcomes of such anti-Black logics and their impact in the realm of the culture industries. Indeed, in Canada current debates concerning the proposed "Memorial to the Victims of Communism—Canada, a Land of Refuge" in Ottawa championed by then Prime Minister Stephen Harper, and similarly the proposed, "privately funded" Mother Canada monument on the East Coast (in an environmentally sensitive national park), alongside the now up and running Canadian Museum for Human Rights in Winnipeg, all in our view represent significant outcomes and losses for a more radical collective possibility of Canada. The then Stephen Harper Conservative government and its neoliberal wealthy backers (in the case of the Canadian Museum of Immigration at Pier 21, the Canadian Museum for Human Rights and the Mother Canada monument, the Asper family), have attempted to re-narrate Canadian history in a number of ways.

Chief among their goals is to unproblematically forge identifications with a singular European past, as the outstretched arms of the proposed Mother Canada monument suggest, especially during and after the First and Second World Wars. This move works in a number of ways to project an image of Canada that the historical record actually does not support. But the institutions also function as sites for a liberal and corporate multiculturalism that reproduces racial hierarchies in numerous ways. For example, the Black presence in all these institutions is extremely limited and largely framed only through twentieth century migrations. Indeed, to do otherwise would call attention to the history of slavery in Canada and even more so to a multicultural policy and rhetoric that obscures a pre-Confederation Black presence and its attendant structural racisms, in favour of a more recent discourse of Canadian benevolence and multicultural inclusion—a benevolence and inclusion that requires forgetting late 19th century racist migration legislation and enforcement that "deemed unsuitable" Black peoples. It is our argument that the very logics and foundations of these institutions draw from historical and contemporary forms of anti-blackness that are so pervasive and diffuse that the logics of their very structure cannot comprehend what is at play and what then is at stake for Black subjecthood and Black lives.

When such logics are extended into the artworld, similar dynamics are at play. We are suggesting that Black Canadian art making relies on an infrastructure that was not designed to make Black art possible in the first instance, because it was fundamentally not structured to make BlackLife possible either. We think this is made clear to any of us who wish to see it now. Nonetheless, if we can be clear about the contexts within which BlackLife and Black art making happen and are produced, we must contend with the late modern capitalist structural anti-blackness that continually seeks to make blackness disappear from anything called Canadian despite claiming otherwise. Therefore, what we might call the reformist (and we don't use that word as a bad word) efforts of the 1980s and 1990s, which meant to produce modes or practices to make Black artists intelligible and recognizable to various art institutions, have significantly run their course and might be marked as failures. Reform is not always and everywhere useless, though; reform can be read as a compromise on to something altogether more promising. Indeed, many cultural institutions could well point to individuals and, for sure, policies and practices coming from that period as sources of learning from the historical past. However, on further investigation something more troubling comes into sight.

Across the cultural industries in Canada, Black work gets some engagement, but truth be told often that engagement is for reasons that produce liberal and corporate multiculturalism to benefit the narrative of a benevolent state and its institutions. Indeed, many an institution believes, for example, that if they show one Black artist then they have done their work, as one noted curator at a university gallery has reportedly said. Similarly, institutions refuse to acknowledge that the scholarly and intellectual apparatus necessary for the intellectual project of Black art making is crucial to its reception. Thus, universities in Canada are also deeply implicated in the problem I am narrating here. The limited number of Black academics is a significant problem, but as well the demands that their work address certain areas also produces forms of engaged non-engagement that buttress the status quo.

CONCLUSION

Indeed, Canada's Black population tends to mirror Black Britain in a number of ways from art to education. The literary scene, mentioned before, mirrors that of Britain. Why the similarity? In 2015, the Black British writer Bernardine Evaristo (African Literature Association Conference, Bayreuth) gave an account of the same time period in Britain, in which a similar dynamic was at play. She too recalled the activism of the 1980s, the burgeoning of work in the 1990s, and its disappearance in the 2000s. She spoke of multiple efforts currently to rebuild and to sustain the public presentation and sustenance of Black artistic contributions in Britain. Evaristo's account is important in that it further indexes how racial capitalism works across the globe and especially in so-called Western metropolises. The American artist Jimmie Durham has pointed out that the contemporary museum practices what he calls "vampirical activities" (p.20). His critique means to alert us to the ways the museum has come to learn to work with its past in the aftermath of the "culture wars" without actually changing its foundations. Vampires only expire when they are totally destroyed, and given that the very foundations of capital, both its economic and ideological underpinnings, are structurally anti-Black, we have no choice left to us but to imagine and put into practice a different world, one in which having to claim Black lives matter is greeted with puzzlement.

Conclusion:
BlackLife...: The Black Test

The Movement for Black Lives has made it imperative that we are specific in our claims concerning Black people and others. So, what are the stakes of living full lives as Black people in Canada? We often find ourselves in a profound state of sadness concerning BlackLife. It is, however, not a sadness that immobilizes, but one that makes us see and witness this world so much more clearly. When one sees more clearly one begins to witness the ways in which discourse and practices of democracy, diversity, inclusion, and a range of ideas meant to interrupt inequality and supposedly produce a different society does not work for Black people. The claim we are making is especially so in regard to formal politics and its machinations. We have been unable to unsee the ways in which liberal, conservative and left discourses continue to fail Black people, constantly endangering our lives not only in Canada but globally as well.

The spectacular deaths of Black people globally are a symptom of a much larger systemic and structural formation that must be undone. The structural formation we want to make clear is that of capitalism and its ongoing production of BlackLife as outside of life and only noticed if commodified. We seek to challenge those committed to the ideals of modernity to take seriously those ideals they espouse, because if they did, those ideals would indeed produce a different kind of world. By this we mean that at the level of policy, politics and the everyday, those who claim to want a more just world and believe it to be possible under this current organization of human life must then work to make modernist ideas complete. As things presently stand collectively human crises of all kinds leave Black lives vulnerable and exposed to some of the most brutal conditions of contemporary life, often culminating in our brutal deaths.

Indeed, we are suggesting that BlackLife seems to be summed up in a cruel arithmetics that position us as both a cost and a deficit simultaneously. These arithmetics are both material and otherwise. The arithmetics of BlackLife is a cruel calculation, hinted at above in the previous chapters, that has its corollary in both debasement of BlackLife and the commodification of it at the same time. Additionally, BlackLife that must encounter the state, again as discussed in these pages, finds itself encumbered in calculations that position it in ways that render it always in precarious positions. Black people are required to count all kinds of things: the numbers of our deaths, the first to accomplish this or that, and so on. These forms of arithmetic that frame BlackLife are strange and marvelous simultaneously.

Take that for example in Canada Black people are dispro-portionately murdered during encounters with state agents and state institutions. Specifically, while Black Torontonians account for merely 8.8% of the overall population, a recent study by the Ontario Human Rights Commission (2018) found "Black people are 20 times more likely than a White person to be involved in a fatal shooting by the Toronto Police Service" (p. 3). So how does this get calculated at the level of the state? One way in which it gets calculated is as blame, as responsibility and a host of other concerns that never fundamentally account for how Black people attempt to survive in a system launched against the very possibil-ity of BlackLife. In this instance BlackLife is deficit.

In its 2018 budget, the Federal government announced it would allocate 19 million dollars to the Public Health Agency of Canada over five years for "culturally relevant mental health programs for Black Canadian communities" (Canadian Heritage, 2018), which was later followed by the September 2018 government announcement to support Black Canadian youth, by investing $9 million over three years, although the government acknowledged this latter pledge was actually the "investment that was originally announced in [the 2018] Budget." These announcements calculate BlackLife as a cost. These "investments" do not and refuse to account for the foundational and fundamental reasons that make BlackLife a life positioned between hopelessness and something more possible. These mea-sures cannot account for a world not made to produce BlackLife as a life necessary to its claims of modernist forms of perfection.

Take as another example, the now Liberal government announcement of funds for Black mental health. Many may query why funds being allocated to Black mental health service provision would be problematic. The simple question is: can these funds or similar "investments" stem the tide of Black death prematurely by the hands of the state? We would argue that such funds and the services that might be provided, simply cannot. However, we must consider the ways in which anti-Black calculations are made against the costs of our lives. More specifically, according to Statistics Canada's latest Census (2016), almost 1.2 million people in Canada are Black—the equivalent of 3.5 % of the country's overall population. Among the 3.5% of Black Canadians, Black youth represent 26.6% or 318,812. Put bluntly, the formulaic response to years of dispossession, degradation, displacement, and the ongoing compounding, and (re)configurations of colonialism(s) and white supremacy that continue to cement Black people at the bottom of every health, social, political and economic indicator, surely cannot be resolved by allotting approximately $15.85 Canadian per Black person or $28.23 per young Black person in this country. Ultimately, what Black people must reckon with vis-à-vis the state is the fact that our historical arrival in the Americas and into the present is not something that can be solved by simple adjustments to the ongoing colonial state.

The existence of the nonhuman in relation to the Canadian State is for purposes of enumeration. Those whose humanity remains in question are incalculable, and to this end, the enumerating of 'black' must not be conflated with the of enumerating of the human, the citizen or the social/political actor. The calculating of 'black' is in reference to the *body* and never the *Black person*, the *human* or our *humanity*. Therefore, how does one construct and calculate care for the nonhuman, more precisely the 'black' enumerated State body? And who are those black bodies?

If we stack up the federal government's 19 million in mental health funding against the city of Toronto's one billion plus budget for policing we see how the calculus of the financialization of human life leaves Black people in precarious situations. We have already noted that policing is one of the most central forces of Black death; we wonder how do those numbers stack up to shift the terrain from death to life for Black peoples? The brutal arithmetics of late modernity continue to discount Black lives in deeply fundamental ways all the while desiring for us to pretend that it is care.

Black people are dying in our cities, crossing oceans, in resource wars not of our making; in every conceivable arena of life we are dying and dying in numbers disproportionate to others. Indeed, it is obvious that Black people's lives are disposable in a way that is radically different from others globally. It is why we want to clearly propose that any new policy actions must pass what we will call the Black Test. The Black Test simply suggests that any policy that does not meet the requirement of ameliorating the dire conditions of Black people's lives is not a policy worth having. This proposal is a challenge to rethink the very grounds of a desired national and global transformative change—where it begins and where it ends. The Black Test is a proposal and a provocation to those committed to modernity's ideals to notice and to urgently act on how encounters with BlackLife always seem to reveal the limits of their policy imaginations. The Black Test requires us to think another and different world now.

We believe that an ethical politics of life demands a radical approach to dissolving inequality or at the least radically ameliorating it. Specifically, in our current political systems, political actors going under the label liberals and the left claim to be desirous and wanting a new world order. We specifically address liberals and the left because both camps claim a desire to speak with, on behalf of and for a sense of community that is bigger than themselves and both camps claim to espouse a politics guided by an ethics that is rooted in justice broadly conceived. But we turn to liberals and the left because their lofty claims have consistently and spectacularly failed Black people in North America and globally while claiming otherwise. Applying the Black Test to their claims makes their political rhetoric rudely clear in regards to BlackLife.

Why is this the case? For us it is very simple and quite clear why liberals and the left fail so spectacularly to address or achieve any traction on the most significant conditions of urgency effecting BlackLife. We claim it is simple, because since the mid-20th century in North America and globally, liberals and the left have wanted to believe that the conditions for Black self-determination have been possible. Liberal and left's joint and collective belief in colour-blind responses to the urgencies of our times is the most significant and fundamental flaw of their politics. It bears repeating continually that whatever the economic, social or cultural markers are, Black people find themselves definitively at the bottom rungs of them, and in Canada always alongside Indigenous peoples. And yet, at the level of government, party politics, think tanks and policy-making more generally, Black people receive little focused political concern. In the corridors of policy-making, political reform debates, mobilization of voters and on and on, a focus on Black people remains absent. This fundamental intellectual failure is what produces a profound sadness for us, a sadness that requires action. We offer and make use of the Black Test to arrive at this analysis.

Let us then state that any contemporary political project that does not clearly address Black people will be a failed political project. In the Canadian context, we cannot adequately deal with unemployment, housing, education, justice and crime, migration, health care and so on without directly engaging Black people and their everyday lives. Liberal and left organizers and policy makers working on the larger context of inequality who do not see Black people as the epicentre of concern will fail to make traction in the ways necessary for us to produce a different nation and eventually a different globe. We do not make this argument based in some notion of Black exceptionalism; we make it based in the routinized evidence that we can see everywhere if we care to notice. In prisons, with children in care, unemployment, low educational achievement levels, health outcomes, the statistics demonstrate Black people's profound levels of disadvantage, to put it mildly. How can we propose and enact new imaginaries for political, social, economic and cultural transformation without specific engagement with the Black population if we are serious about change?

How is it not clear to those who work for a different world that a focus on inequality through the evidence and experience of Black people would have to be the foundation upon which radical and actual transformative change is possible? We want to suggest that liberals' and the left's banal commitments to white supremacy and its racial hierarchies, which place Black people at the bottom everywhere and on every measure, is fundamental to the answer. The unseen commitment to white supremacist logics means that even those claiming a commitment to change unconsciously act out of a negation to blackness and Black people. This political negation remains a dire aspect of our politics for a desired transformation. This political negation requires a new imaginary structure and logic. In short, a transformation of what is imaginable by the liberal and left political logics of our day is urgently necessary. And to achieve it liberal and left political logics will have to invent ways of undoing and destroying the ways in which a routinized white supremacist logic frames our contemporary movements still, including those of anti-racism and social justice formations.

In broader terms than liberal and left politics we are in a kind of stalemate in our current global arrangements. Black intellectuals' contributions to global life remain either ignored or briefly fetishized, only to be quickly replaced by some logic that both draws for it and simultaneously undermines it. It is for that reason that we insist that every policy proposal should be exposed to the Black Test. By that we mean it should meet the test of ameliorating Black dispossession and making BlackLife possible. If the policy does not meet the Black Test, then it is a failed policy, always already, from the first instance of its proposal.

Finally, the kind of political logic that we are calling for requires a different understanding of the world and a new imaginary that exceeds this world, as we presently know it, experience it and live it. Black intellectuals have been leading us to this new imaginary for a long time, in a sustained fashion since our arrival in the Americas. We are now fully faced with the challenge of how to hear them and institute their knowledges for continued global life.

References

Austin, D. (2013). *Fear of a black nation: Race, sex, and security in sixties Montreal*. Toronto, ON: Between the Lines.

Baldwin, J. (1963). *The fire next time*. New York, NY: Dial Press.

Barrett, L. (1999). *Blackness and value: Seeing double*. Cambridge, MA: Cambridge University Press.

Bauman, Z. (2004). *Wasted lives: Modernity and its outcasts*. Cambridge, MA: Polity.

Boyce Davies, C. (2008). *Left of Karl Marx: The political life of black communist Claudia Jones*. Durham, NC: Duke University Press.

Brand, D. (1997). *Land to light on*. Toronto, ON: McClelland & Stewart.

Brand, D. (2001). *A map to the door of no return: Notes to belonging*. Toronto, ON: Doubleday Canada.

Brand, D. (2002). *Thirsty*. Toronto, ON: McClelland & Stewart.

Brand, D. (2005). *What we all long for: A novel*. Toronto, ON: Alfred A. Knopf Canada.

Canadian Heritage. (2018). The Government of Canada announces new funding for black Canadian youth. Retrieved from https://www.canada.ca/en/canadian-heritage/news/2018/06/the-government-of-canada-announces-new-funding-for-black-canadian-youth.html

Clarke, A. (2008). *More: A novel*. Markham, ON: Thomas Allen Publishers.

Derrida, J. (1994). *Specters of Marx: The state of the debt, the work of mourning, and the new international.* New York, NY: Routledge.

Durham, Jimmie. (1990) Cowboys and . . . Indians. *Third Text 12.*

Eber, D. (1969). *The computer centre party: Canada meets black power.* Montreal, QC: Tundra Books.

Fanon, F. (1963). *The wretched of the earth.* New York, NY: Grove Press.

Fatona, A. M. (2011). "Where outreach meets outrage": Racial equity at the Canada council for the arts (1989 – 1999). University of Toronto Doctor of Philosophy Thesis

Forsythe, D. (1971). *Let the niggers burn.* Montreal, QC: Black Rose Books.

Foster, C. (2002). *A place called heaven: The meaning of being black in Canada.* Toronto, ON: HarperCollins.

Foucault, M. (1979). *Discipline and punish: The birth of the prison.* New York, NY: Vintage Books.

Gilroy, P. (2000). *Against race: Imagining political culture beyond the color line.* Cambridge, MA: Belknap Press of Harvard University Press.

Gilroy, P. (2000) "The sugar you stir". P. Gilroy, L. Grossberg & A. McRobbie (Ed). *Without guarantees: In honour of Stuart Hall.* London: Verso.

Gordon, A. (1997). *Ghostly matters: Haunting and the sociological imagination.* Minneapolis: University of Minnesota Press.

Grant, G. (1965). *Lament for a nation: The defeat of Canadian nationalism.* Montreal, QC and Kingston ON: Mcgill-Queen's University Press.

Hall, S., Critcher, C., Jefferson, T., Clarke, J. and Roberts, B. (2013) *Policing the crisis: Mugging, the state and law and order*. London, UK: Palgrave McMillan.

Jordan, J. (1992) The craft that politics requires: An interview with June Jordan. (M. Christakos, Interviewer). *Fireweed: A Feminist Quarterly 36* (Summer): pp. 26-39.

Kwamdela, O. (1971). *Niggers ... this is Canada*. Toronto: 21st Century Book.

Lewis, S. (1992, June 9). Report of the advisor on race relations to the Premier of Ontario, Bob Rae. Retrieved from the website of the Ontario Special Investigations Unit, www.siu.on.ca/pdfs/report_of_the_advisor_on_race_relations_to_the_ premier_of_ontario_bob_rae.pdf

McKittrick, K. (2017). Worn out. *Southeastern Geographer, 57:1*, (2017): 96-100.

Mignolo, W. (2005). *The idea of Latin America*. Malden, MA: Blackwell Publishing.

Mills, C. (1997). *The racial contract*. Ithaca, NY: Cornell University Press.

Morrison, T. (1992). *Playing in the dark: Whiteness and the literary imagination*. Cambridge, MA: Harvard University Press.

Nas, J. (2008). Black President [recorded as Nas]. On *Untitled*. New York, NY: Def Jam Recordings.

Offishall, K. (2005). Fire and Glory [recorded as Kardinal Offishall]. On *Fire and Glory*. EMI Canada.

Ong, A. (2006). *Neoliberalism as exception: Mutations in citizenship and sovereignty*. Durham, NC: Duke University Press.

Philip, M. N. (1996). Why multiculturalism can't end racism. In M.N. Philip (Ed.), *Frontiers: essays and writings 1984-1992* (pp.181-186). Stratford, ON: The Mercury Press. (Original work published 1992)

Roberts, A. (2005). *A view for freedom: Alfie Roberts speaks.* Montreal: Institute.

Robinson, C. J. (2000) *Black marxism: The making of the black radical tradition.* Chapel Hill, NC: University of North Carolina Press.

Said, E. (1993). *Culture and imperialism.* New York, NY: Vintage Books

Smallwood, T., & Almonte, R. (2000). *A narrative of Thomas Smallwood (coloured man).* Toronto, ON: Mercury Press.

Walcott, R. (2000). Rude: Contemporary black Canadian cultural criticism. Toronto: Insomniac Press.

Walcott, R. (2001). Caribbean pop culture in canada: Or, the impossibility of belonging to the nation. *Small Axe*, (9), 123.

Walcott, R. (2003). *Black like who?: Writing black canada* (2nd rev. ed.). Toronto: Insomniac Press.

Walcott, R. (2004). Dramatic instabilities: Diasporic aesthetics as a question for and about nation. *Canadian Theatre Review*, 118(118), 99.

Walcott, R. (2006) Salted cod...: Black Danada and diasporic sensibilities. *Reading the Image* 2006: pp. 14-20.

Walcott, R. (2014). The book of others (book IV): Canadian multiculturalism, the state, and its political legacies. *Canadian Ethnic Studies*, 46(2), 127-132. doi:10.1353/ces.2014.0018

Walcott, R. (2018). Freedom now suite: Black feminist turns of voice. *Small Axe*, 22(3), 151-159.

Welsh, Moira. 1992. Authorities Were Expecting Peaceful Demonstration. *The Toronto Star*, May 5, Retrieved October 15, 2012 (http://micromedia. pagesofthepast.ca/PageView.asp).

Wilderson, F. (2010). *Red, white and black: Cinema and the structure of U.S. antagonisms*. Durham: Duke University Press.

Wynter, S. (1992). Rethinking "aesthetics": Notes towards a deciphering practice. M. Cham (Ed) *Ex-Iles: Essays on Caribbean Cinema*. Trenton, NJ: Africa World Press.

Wynter, S. (1994). NO HUMANS INVOLVED: An Open Letter To My Colleagues. *Forum N.H.I.: Knowledge for the 21st Century. 1*, no. 1, Fall.

Wynter, S. (1995). but what does "wonder" do? meaning, canons, too? on literary, on cultural context, and what it's like to be one/not one of us. *SEHR 4*, Issue 1.

Biographies

Professor Rinaldo Walcott is the Director of the Women & Gender Studies Institute. Rinaldo's research is founded in a philosophical orientation that is concerned with the ways in which coloniality shapes human relations across social and cultural time and focuses on Black cultural politics; histories of colonialism in the Americas, multiculturalism, citizenship, and diaspora; gender and sexuality; and social, cultural and public policy.

Idil Abdillahi is an Assistant Professor in the School of Social Work at Ryerson University. As a critical interdisciplinary scholar, she has published on a wide array of topics such as: mental health, policing, poverty, HIV/AIDS, organizational development, and several other key policy areas at the intersection of BlackLife and state interruption. Most notably, Idil's cutting-edge research on Blackened madness and anti-Black sanism has informed the current debates on fatal police shootings of Black mad identified people.